Sam Rockwell
Forward by **Jerry Cook**

LEADING BY
BEING & DOING

Integrating
Person & Practice
in Ministry

Published by Encounters Press
Inspiring Vision, Fulfilling Dreams, Publishing Excellence
Tulsa, Oklahoma, U.S.A.
Printed in U.S.A.

In a world plagued by conflict, rapid change, and relentless pressures, we need books to help us unravel the confusion in an attempt to make sense of life.

The printed books, ebooks and other media published under the banner of **Encounters Press** are targeted to be on the front-lines. As publishers we want to be responsive to the issues that touch people's lives. One of our primary missions is to publish true human experiences reflecting tragedy to triumph, underdog victories and conquests over the impossible. Additionally, **Encounters Press i**s providing church leaders with biblical, user-friendly materials that will assist them in their evangelistic, teaching, leadership training and discipleship efforts.

For a FREE CATALOG of resources from *Encounters Press* **please call your Christian supplier or email us at: Publisher@EncountersPress.com.**

Back cover photo courtesy of Lancia E. Smith Photography.

www.lanciaEsmith.com

TABLE of CONTENTS

part 1
Being

part 2
Doing

dedication

This book is dedicated to church planters and their families.
All proceeds will go to a church planters development fund.

A special thanks to Lancia Smith.

forward
by Jerry Cook

Being and doing do not apportion themselves evenly in life. They seem to pendulum back and forth. We set a time aside for prayer and inner development; then suddenly frenetic demand imposes itself on our days and weeks with no relief. Not only the demands of people, which are constant, but the demands of opportunities that only come once and have a limited window of time for response.

Then the demands of crises, which never make an appointment but suddenly present themselves at our doorstep and cannot be ignored or delegated. We must act and it seems every act imposes new demands.

We may plunge on recklessly, comforting ourselves with that

mythical "sometime soon" when we will take a little time for our family and ourselves. Often, before the "sometime" arrives, we find ourselves shriveling inwardly. Our life narrows into role-play with little substance. Schedules mock us and time management skills forsake our most noble efforts. With an impoverished being and unrelenting doing we become fragile shells which will ultimately implode.

Integrating being and doing brings life into focus. Their pursuit is demanded and their understanding essential to our Christian life and especially for the Christian leader. *They must never be separated or inverted.* To put doing before being, or to separate them into different compartments leads to disaster.

Doing must flow seamlessly out of being. Leaders ultimately minister who they are, not just what they say. If our character is weak or flawed, those weaknesses and flaws will be reflected in our actions and choices. The biblical principle applies here; "Out of the heart the mouth speaks." Jesus teaches us that evil acts flow from evil hearts. A sick inner being corrupts the noblest act.

He shows us further, that to be clean but empty inwardly is also disastrous. The room left empty by the exit of one demon is soon inhabited by seven more. The issue is not the pursuit of inner perfection. That is just a relocated legalism. Rather, it is both a cleansed and indwelt inner being. Ours must not be a heart cleansed and proudly dated as to the time of its cleansing as though a past event insures present cleanliness. Inner rooms do not stay empty or clean. That is the frustration of legalism.

Cultivating the conscious awareness of His inner presence is the sole focus of being. It is out of this conscious, constant awareness that everything else flows. Jesus taught us, "If you love me (being) keep my commandments (doing)." Leading in the Kingdom is not a matter of technique; it is rather a focused relationship that leads to unquestioned and at times unprecedented obedience.

Herein lies the futility of constantly searching for a model for leadership or church. It is not a matter of precedence. It does not matter if what you are doing has ever been done before or if it will ever be done again. What matters is that you are acting out of obedience to the inner voice of Jesus. All doing, all technique must be forged out of this inner presence and loving relationship.

Yet we are not growing when we monastically isolate ourselves in devotional study and exercise. Nor are we growing when we are frantically fulfilling some religious duty. *We are growing only when both the being and the doing are seamlessly engaged. The greater awareness of His presence does not lead to more contemplation. It leads to obedience. And obedience leads to a greater sense of His presence.*

What has this to do with leadership? Everything. If we lead out of an awareness of His presence we will lead our followers into an awareness of His presence. I understand this result to be the great purpose of all our leading.

It is to this end that this book is dedicated. Sam has included excellent technique, but if that is all we are looking for that will be all we see. In that case, we may be helped, but we will miss the true depth of the book and the essence of its message.

Sam Rockwell is not merely a theoretician. He speaks from an active and multi-faceted life and ministry. He is a university professor, a pastor, and a District Supervisor for the pastors of his denomination. He is a scholar and expert in the area of institutions, their dynamics and development. Sam comes to this book with a broad and highly practical perspective. His viewpoint, advice and insight will enrich the reader and assist in striking the needed balance between being and doing.

introduction

This book, as the title suggests, is both personal and practical. "Personal" in that the first chapters are written from an introspective point of view as I attempt to explore my questions, challenges, and pain through the Biblical stories of Jacob, Peter, Hannah, and Moses. I invite you, the reader, to enter in to these narratives and supply your own experience and struggles as a form of interpreting for yourself what God is saying to you about who you are and who you might become. It is an attempt to blend my thoughts and story with yours and those of the characters in the Scripture to penetrate to the issue of what it is to "be" a person of faith, and perhaps even a leader of others.

This book is also practical in that the second half is written mostly as a response to very real dilemmas and questions spiritual leaders grapple with on a daily basis: What am I supposed to be accomplishing? How is this measured? What will last over time? How do I start? These "lessons" were originally drawn-up on a napkin usually during a breakfast meeting with a fellow pastor or leader. We were attempting to get to the heart of a particular problem, and together, an essential instruction was crafted. So the latter section of the book is an attempt to reach some basic understanding of what ministry is in a measurable and concrete way in contrast to the first section of the book, which is meant to unearth questions, which only you, the reader, can answer.

Combining "being and doing" suggests that life is a whole experience not a compartmentalized set of activities performed by a "ministry machine" or a "holy robot." Ministry is a total life, not just a spiritualized form of a production line. We know this is true, of course, but modern culture often creates the illusion that life fits neatly into units and "slots," when in fact, it doesn't. Our fast paced lives may leave us feeling like we are disconnected from ourselves; we may experience a niggling sense of dissonance between who we are, authentically, and what we run around doing impulsively. These pages are a reminder that our lives may potentially become more generative and positively self-reinforcing and not characterized by misfires, fitful starts and stops, and frantic activity.

The chapters of this book are woven together with the following three practices in mind. These "ways of being" connect the inner person who communes with God and the outer person who "gets things done" in the everyday world. These practices describe a "being and doing" kind of wisdom that provides the framework for this book:

Being Reflective: We learn when we make new connections between new information, new experiences, and things we already know. Learning is about the relationships between things, not just the things themselves. That's why there is value in learning what might not seem immediately applicable. Wisdom is generated when *we see on our own* relationships between things and this usually requires an additional step of reflection and an added quality of personal curiosity. Connecting disciplines, subjects, and ideas, whether in the fields of art, literature, gardening, theology, or motorcycle maintenance, grounding them in personal experience, and arriving at a deeper appreciation of relationships of all kinds, distinguishes wisdom from mere knowledge. This kind of attitude allows us to suspend judgment for a season, to listen vulnerably, and "be" present in new circumstances with openness to be genuinely changed, not merely informed. "Being," suggests that learning and growing are more a state of play than of over-serious work, more a connection to "who" I am becoming than "what" I do performing my role in life.

Being in Community: Learning with others accelerates and optimizes learning. People learn best when the lines between teacher and student are fuzzy so that true discovery can occur; when we are simultaneously "giving" and "receiving" knowledge, and the learning is "between us" not just "deposited" in us. The social component of the learning equation acknowledges that wisdom is emergent, which means it arises as new and uniquely "situated" knowledge. True learning is not just old information re-hashed; it is freshly constructed vision for the current moment. This kind of immediate relevance only occurs when learning is a dynamic creation of mutual exchange. Again, "playing as learning" is to blur the lines between work and play, between my current self-image and "someone" new, between what I think I know, and what threatens my self-competency. This is the essence of a life committed to learning and leading.

Being by Doing: Learning is achieved when it is enacted in the real world. As a "pentecostal," I believe in the seamless merging of the spiritual and the physical, the Kingdom of God and present reality; and the healing of the outer as well as the inner person. Moreover, I believe that belief and action are one organic whole. *"We have to understand,"* said biologist and philosopher, Jacob Bronowski, *"that the world can only be grasped by action, not by contemplation alone. [That] the hand is more important than the eye...[that] the hand is the cutting edge of the mind."* [1] Learning as a way of changing, means that we embrace "learning for the sheer sake of learning" because there is always a connection between new information and our current situation, whether we can immediately discern it or not. However, learning is intensely condensed when it combines deep reflection, mutual give and take, and common goals which require the embodiment of wisdom into personal, and especially, collective, action.

To learn as a way of changing is to bring oneself into the entire experience of life so that learning is embedded into everything that one is and does. Perhaps to lead is to be privileged in any given situation and moment to be the most thoughtful, relational, and purposeful person in the room. ⌇

Who I am
forms and defines what I do.
What I do
forms and defines who I am,
creating my identity.

When I am vulnerable
in my community
and disciplined
in my reflection,
I can be assured of continually
becoming who I am.
–Sam Rockwell

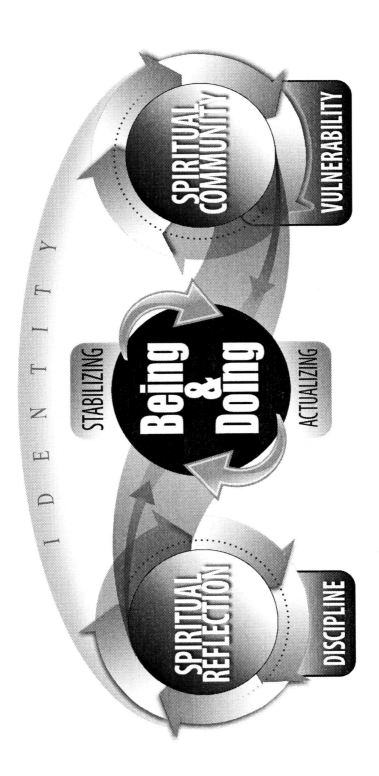

When you <u>stabilize</u> your actions
with a deep sense
of spiritual identity,
you will be selective
and focused.
–Sam Rockwell

PART 1

Being
Stabilizes Doing

identity

When the dust settles and the light of day
dawns, Jacob is left with a new name
and a permanently sustained injury.
Both of these add up to
an odd yet remarkable blessing.
–Sam Rockwell

Self as Instrument

The Transforming Power of a Surrendered Life

Then the messengers returned to Jacob, saying,
"We came to your brother Esau, and he also is coming to meet you,
And four hundred men are with him." So Jacob was greatly afraid and distressed...

—GENESIS 32:3-6

*J*acob has lived his whole life as the underdog who breaks the rules to get what he wants. He is a schemer. He knows all the angles. He lives by his wits. He is tricky Jake.

> *Then Jacob was left alone; and a Man wrestled with him until the breaking of day. Now when He saw that He did not prevail against him, He touched the socket of his hip; and the socket of Jacob's hip was out of joint as He wrestled with him. And He said, "Let Me go, for the day breaks."*

> *But he said, "I will not let You go unless You*
> *bless me!"*
> *So He said to him, "What is your name?"*
> *He said, "Jacob."*
> *And He said, "Your name shall no longer be called*
> *Jacob, but Israel; for you have struggled with God*
> *and with men, and have prevailed."*
> *Then Jacob asked, saying, "Tell me Your name,*
> *I pray."*
> *And He said, "Why is it that you ask about My*
> *name?" And He blessed him there.*
> *So Jacob called the name of the place Peniel: "For I*
> *have seen God face to face, and my life is preserved."*
> *Just as he crossed over Peniel the sun rose on him,*
> *and he limped on his hip.* —Genesis 32:24-31

Jacob outmaneuvered his father Isaac and outfoxed his brother Esau. He managed to get rich and get the girl too. Along the way, he gets a taste of his own medicine when his father-in-law, Laban, tricks him into working for seven extra years for his beloved Rachel after hoodwinking him into marrying her older sister, Leah. (Surely Jacob understood a little how he had made Esau feel when he woke up from his wedding night with the wrong bride in his arms! Whoa!)

Despite these setbacks and turnabouts, Jacob's calculating

and wily nature persists.

He is, as he has always been, a man with a plan. And now after having gained a fortune and two wives he leaves Laban and returns home to claim his place as heir to his father. More than anything else, he wants the blessing and legitimacy of his family heritage. In packing his bags and loading up his family and possessions to return home, Jacob is being true and consistent to his lifelong prevailing characteristic: personal confidence. He is self-assured in his ability to make it work. Yes, he is guilty of misrepresenting himself to his father and taking advantage of the weakness of his brother. Yes, he is guilty of escaping from the consequences of his trickery without a word. Yes, he is guilty of allowing his fawning mother to aid and abet his cowardice.

No matter. He will pursue what he wants. This is his way.

For his entire life, he has depended on his cleverness and charming personality to get him out of trouble. Somehow, he will return home and face his father and brother. He will face the music.

If one is to accomplish anything in life it does require confidence. But to experience God's best, to become what one is created to be in the fullest sense means to transcend personal confidence in one's plans and place confidence in God's presence. This is the lesson of Jacob's wrestling match with God.

Jacob's world was rocked when he heard these few words, *"Esau is coming to meet you, and four hundred men are with him."* Suddenly his confidence is shattered and he spirals into panic. All of his worst fears have abruptly blown up in his face. He is undone.

SOMETIMES GOD USES OUR WORST FEARS TO PREPARE AND POSITION US FOR AN ENCOUNTER WITH HIM.

Maybe you have experienced an unexpected loss of some kind, a death or divorce or even the loss of your job. A few years ago, I experienced something I never thought could happen to me. I was facing the specter of a divorce. No matter what I did, no matter how I resisted, I could see that I could not change its inevitability. I could not conceive that this could happen to me and my marriage, and yet it was upon me. I felt victimized and helpless to change what I felt I should have some power to control. I was left to stew in my fears and despair. It felt like my life had ended. It felt like my future was suddenly cut-short. My imagination took over and I prepared myself for all the worst possible outcomes. I was undone.

It is the mirage of total loss that sometimes creates the necessary conditions for God to get our attention and teach us life-altering lessons. This was certainly true in Jacob's case.

As the sun slowly fades, and all of Jacob's family members and possessions have gone on ahead of him, evidently to "soften" Esau, Jacob is left alone with his thoughts. As he is looking off into the distance, perhaps lost in contemplation over his uncertain fate, a mysterious figure emerges from the shadows. This murky character engages Jacob in a body-to-body duel.

The dark figure is strangely familiar to Jacob. He is of equal strength and weight. The physical contest between them is aggressive and spirited, but Jacob never feels imperiled. The unknown combatant matches his every move, shadows his efforts, and yet never finally overcomes him.

Wresting
with God
and wrestling
with self
are often
the same
struggle.

The night and the fight seem to take on an eerie ebb and flow.

JACOB WRESTLES WITH GOD AND HIMSELF

When the dust settles and the light of day dawns, Jacob is left with a new name and a permanently sustained injury. Both of these add up to an odd and remarkable blessing.

Amazingly, I have been able to see the light in my own tunnel. I was not able to forestall my divorce, and I will not recount the story here, but like Jacob, I was both permanently wounded and remarkably restored. What felt like a permanent state of anger has somehow morphed into hope and anticipation for something better. A pervading sense of failure has given way to a willingness to accept and even embrace what I cannot change. I am permanently wounded perhaps, but not mortally so. I can live with a limp.

It is often the most difficult and painful experiences that forge in us the necessary "state of heart" that prepares us for new seasons of leadership and ministry. Leadership is not easily condensed into a few qualities or characteristics. Like Jacob, it is the result of a process of wrestling with God, wrestling with self, confronting our true identity and coming to terms with our wounds.

Jacob's long night of struggle, has for me, come to represent spiritual processes that I can readily identify with. There are several inner transformations that I see emerging from Jacob's wrestling match with God as well as a few insights I am suggesting as a result of my own experience struggling with God.

Wresting with God and wrestling with self are often the same struggle.

It is very interesting that Jacob wrestles with someone who is his physical equal. He is evenly matched. I am speculating, but I think the reason that Jacob's sparring partner is so closely matched with him is because Jacob is struggling with himself as much as he is struggling with God.

God places in our hearts a tiny seed. It is a whispering reminder of what we are called to be. It is often so small and so delicate that it hardly seems real at all. It is not real or powerful enough to really impact our lives, our plans, or our programs for success. Not real, at least until we face some crisis that forces us to come to terms with what we really believe about ourselves and our best possible future.

Perhaps our wrestling with God is precipitated by our latent beliefs about ourselves. These latent beliefs are the stirrings created by this tiny seed. We have a nobler self that is waiting in the wings but we are unable to summons it on our own. We are unable to change our own nature and unable to be what we really want to be.

When my situation became reality, I spent many nights awake, grappling with things that I had said and done that I regretted. One night when I was feeling particularly lonely and desperate, I called a dear friend for solace because I thought he'd commiserate with me. He sympathized but did not coddle. We had a conversation that I will never forget. I can still hear his voice as he gently asked me a few questions that helped me, over time, penetrate the fog of confusion and frustration:

"What kind of person are you, really?" he asked.

"How do you want to emerge from this experience?"

"Could it be that the way you handle yourself now may determine the definition of your character?"

"How do you want to be defined?"

Up to that point I had been wrestling with God about my circumstances, my fears, my emotional pain, and my future. What God was wrestling with me about was how I was going to define myself. As this personal ordeal unfolded in my life, I learned how to surrender. I experienced a peace and calm, not because my situation had changed but because I realized what the real issues needed to be for me.

The paradoxical thing about letting God change you is that

_____ ❦ _____

It is not our

cleverness

that makes

a lasting impact;

It is our

"unadorned self."

_____

when you surrender your personal agendas and fears, you are then in a good position to embrace the deepest and best aspirations you have for yourself. By letting go of yourself, you possess yourself as never before.

There is another paradox that is indicative of having a true encounter with God while struggling with Him. At the moment that you feel most challenged and most confronted by God, when you feel most overwhelmed by your personal failures, and when feelings of regret almost sweep you under, you also feel overcome with a deep sense of acceptance. Paul Tillich writes,

It is as though a voice were saying, "you are

accepted, you are accepted! Accepted by that which is greater than you, and the name of which you do not know. Do not ask for the name now; perhaps you will find it later. Do not try to do anything now; perhaps you will do much. Do not seek for anything; do not intend anything. Simply accept the fact that you are accepted. [2]

This is the essence of an encounter with God and the essence of grace. Jacob is asked by the mysterious wrestler, "What is your name?" The question forces us to squarely face who we are and who we can become all in the same moment. Only a ruthlessly honest confession of who we are liberates us to accept a whole new vision of what we may become. Now Jacob would bear his new name meaningfully.

It is not our cleverness that makes a lasting impact; it is our "unadorned self."

Jacob has always been armed with a strategy. His approach to difficulty and opportunity has been to utilize a better plan than the next guy. He is the master chess player, seeing the players and each of their possible moves in advance. So God arranges a kind of competitive event for this tactician; a "match" to engage Jacob's attention. The language of leverage and positioning is one that Jacob understands well. It is his stock-in-trade.

We all have our personal stratagems for getting what we want and need. There isn't anything particularly wrong with this, although sometimes Jacob's approach to getting what he wanted was unethical. It is normal and reasonable to use coping behaviors to get through difficulty. It is normal and reasonable to plan ahead and get the upper hand on circumstances. It is normal and reasonable to use one's natural abilities to succeed.

A crisis arises, however, when God calls on us to surrender our usual tactics for success in our service to Him. He is not impressed with our skills. Don't get me wrong. We are expected to use all our talents and gifts to serve God, but true spiritual leadership and ministry is much more than the mobilization of our talents. It is as much a sacrifice of our talents and skills as the utilization of them.

When faced with the task of accomplishing the impossible for God, our gifts and talent don't matter. So while we are to employ our abilities in God's service, ultimately they must be surrendered to God for Him to get what He is after. And He is after our essential self. God is interested in doing what is beyond the reach of human effort and competence. The business of redemption, spiritual restoration, personal and social transformation is His terrain and it is accomplished through the instruments of surrendered people, not clever plans.

Jacob hobbled to his next appointment. When he met up with Esau the next day it was not with a swagger and a handshake, it was with a wounded body and yielded spirit. And yet he was stronger than he had ever been.

Henri Nouwen, writing about his experiences in L'Arche, a community for mentally handicapped people, talks about the vital experience of simply bringing oneself to the people one serves.

> These broken, wounded and completely unpretentious people forced me to let go of my relevant self – the self that can do things, show things, prove things, build things – and forced me to reclaim that unadorned self in which I am completely vulnerable, open to receive and give love regardless of any accomplishments.[3]

I find myself spending less time preparing for difficult conversations and potentially explosive confrontations. I used to brace myself much more for people; prepare my defense strategy; think and rethink possible answers and retorts. Jacob had learned in his encounter with the wrestler that he could face Esau non-defensively. He could offer himself to others in the same way he had offered himself to God. And no matter what the outcome, he could trust that he would be safe.

My interactions with people have changed. I don't rehearse as much. I trust myself to be honest and to express the feeling I am experiencing in the moment to be enough. I allow conversations and people to unfold. I bring my whole self and try to leave my presuppositions and preplanned agendas in temporary suspension. Surrendering to God results in surrendering our precious preconceived notions of what people are. Jacob had to face Esau as an unadorned and unprotected brother.

Jacob's approach made all the difference. Esau and Jacob were reconciled.

The heart of the matter is to face our greatest challenges openly and non-defensively. Only a wounded and yet healed heart can do this. Only great strength tempered with restraint can do this. Only one who is willing to take on the servant's towel and surrender the

True spiritual leadership and ministry is much more than the mobilization of our talents.

cloaks of personal competency can do this. From God's perspective, our limitations and wounds are our best assets. It is the stuff He can use. It is the substance of miracles.

GOD RESPECTS OUR STRUGGLE

I am struck by how much latitude God gives Jacob to fail and learn. The fact that Jacob wrestled all night says much about God's nature. It says much about his patience with us. This long, exhausting physical contest for position is evidence of God's great respect for those who wrestle with Him. I was on the wrestling team in high school and there is nothing more grueling than the contest for position, which is what wrestling is all about.

Obviously God could have pinned Jacob in the first round. If God were interested in merely winning He could have accomplished that without sweat. God was not trying to win anything, however. He was attempting to engage Jacob's restless soul in a process of self-surrender and self-discovery. He was not trying to vanquish Jacob; he was beckoning Jacob to offer himself willingly and completely. God renames Jacob, but Jacob must embrace his new identity for himself.

God is patient and respectful of our struggle because he sees us as his instruments. It is worth the wait to Him. It is not His way to merely utilize our abilities. He wants to use us. We are the tools of His trade. Charles Spurgeon, in *Lectures to My Students* says,

> *Michelangelo, the elect of the fine arts, understood so well the importance of his tools, that he always made his own brushes with his own hands, and in this he gives us an illustration of the God of grace, who with special care fashions for himself all true ministers.*[4]

When we see for the first time the fathomless forbearance and reverential patience that God has for the process it takes for us to relinquish ourselves to Him fully, it should give us pause.

It should deeply instill in us a willingness to allow others room to fail and learn. It should embed in us a sense of gratitude so thoroughly and profoundly that our mere presence in people's lives elicits in them an overwhelming desire to worship. ☙

personal response

1. In retrospect, list 2 or 3 situations when you remember wrestling with God and yourself. Describe these experiences and how they affected your life.

2. On a scale from 1-10, how difficult is it for you to lay aside your giftings and talents when God is requiring it of you? Explain.

3. Describe what "unadorned self" means to you.

....

....

....

....

....

....

....

....

....

....

engagement

Instead of fretting about getting everything
done, why not simply accept that being
alive means having things to do? Then drop
into full engagement with whatever you're
doing, and let the worry go.
−Martha Beck

Chapter 2

Being Present
Participating in Your Own Life

*T*his story is the most intimate and personal of Jesus' post-resurrection appearances. It is filled with apprehension and expectation because despite all the earth-shaking events that have taken place and despite all the dramatic possibilities that accompany the presence of the risen Christ, it centers on the betrayal of a friendship and its potential for restoration.

> *So when they had eaten breakfast, Jesus said to Simon Peter, "Simon, son of Jonah, do you love Me more than these?"*
>
> *He said to Him, "Yes, Lord; You know that I love*

You."

He said to him, "Feed My lambs."

He said to him again a second time, "Simon, son of Jonah, do you love Me?"

He said to Him, "Yes, Lord; You know that I love You."

He said to him, "Tend My sheep."

He said to him the third time, "Simon, son of Jonah, do you love Me?" Peter was grieved because He said to him the third time, "Do you love Me?"

And he said to Him, "Lord, You know all things; You know that I love You."

Jesus said to him, "Feed My sheep."
                    —John 21: 15-17

Jesus' offer of fellowship in the shadow of Peter's betrayal is moving but not at all sentimental. It is basic and simple in its intent: Jesus prepares a meal for his friend and offers him forgiveness and a pathway to healing.

With a few master strokes, Jesus devastates Peter and rehabilitates him at the same time. He ruins Peter's surface self-assurance, but clears a path for him to discover true spiritual significance.

Jesus does not intend to humiliate Peter but to help him define for himself the true cost and benefit of spiritual intimacy. This elegant and minimal exchange between Jesus and Peter identifies a host of complex questions and issues involved in pursuing a life of ministry. Jesus cuts through Peter's bravado and gets to the real point by identifying for Peter (and for us) at least three important issues: First, the question of love and personal vulnerability; second, the question of belonging and identification; and third, the question of healing and restoration.

We are asked to "place ourselves" squarely in our own lives.

BEING FULLY AWAKE

Love is all about paying attention, being fully present in one's own life, and subsequently being fully "awake" to those God has given us to love. In a culture of multitasking and perpetual diversion, this is a significant challenge.

Not long ago I was interviewing a young seminary student who was interested in finding a place to serve in my district. We had lunch together and had a nice conversation about his spiritual gifts, his ministry, and his family background. I enjoyed hearing his personal story and felt charged by his idealistic fervor. As we finished and I grabbed the bill, he said, "That wasn't so bad."

"I don't bite." I smiled.

"Ya, it's just that your administrative assistant told me you might seem a little distracted."

I laughed and told him that I hoped he felt I cared for him and that I enjoyed our time together. We shook hands and left the restaurant.

It was sometime later that week that his comment struck me as something that I should think about further. I realized that my assistant's harmless "warning" to him was an important (though unintentional) signal to me. Not just because I needed to learn to listen more attentively but that I needed to pay attention to *everything* more attentively. Over a period of a week or so, I could not escape the feeling

---

I was
a distracted
person
in more
ways than
one

that my failure to be a good listener was a deeper problem than I first acknowledged. I was a distracted person in more ways than one. I was not paying close attention to my family. I was not listening to God. I was not connecting with my own thoughts and desires. I was not fully participating in my own life!

I needed to learn to focus on people the very moment they start talking to me. I also needed to become more approachable. A greater challenge, however, was pressing me; the urgency to fundamentally reorient myself. My lack of listening was only a symptom of a much bigger problem. I was not firmly planted in my own life. I was skimming the surface of my experiences and this was inhibiting my ability to really love anyone fully.

James Joyce describes one of his characters as "living a short distance away from his body." I have been tempted to live my life in such a way that it doesn't require my full commitment. I find myself not able to feel my feelings as they occur. Instead, I store them up so that when they do burst out when I am under stress I have no idea what they mean or where they came from. I find myself "living a short distance" from my heart.

No less than three times does Jesus ask Peter this penetrating question: "Do you love me?" I don't think Jesus needed to be affirmed. I don't think Jesus was looking for sentimentality or a particular emotional response from Peter. I think he was asking Peter to thoroughly examine his life. He was creating a lens through which Peter could scrutinize his commitments and his level of awareness. "What do you believe Peter? What are you truly committed to? What are you all about?"

Jesus was asking Peter to pay attention.

When faced with my distracted approach to life, a version of Jesus' conversation plays out in my head:

"Sam, do you love me?"

"I'm doing my best. I'm planning and effectively managing my time and energy for the best possible results."

"Do you love me?"

"I am serving you and a lot of others as well. I have much to do. All of it is worthwhile."

"Do you love me?"

"It's difficult to be entirely present. I have several things going simultaneously." And so on.

When Peter heard the haunting sound of a rooster crow, it was a wake-up call of the highest order. He knew instantaneously, viscerally even, that his life was out of order and that his outbursts of anger and frustration were spiritual problems, not just momentary flare-ups. When things get dropped or neglected in our lives, it may be more than a mere oversight in our personal digital organizer. It may be a sign that we no longer "inhabit" our lives. We may not be wholeheartedly embracing the commitments we make and therefore we are not living in harmony with our authentic selves. We experience a "disconnect" with God and with our mission in life. We cannot love when we are not fully present. Frederick Buechner, in his spiritual autobiography, *Now and Then*, recommends listening at a deeper level:

> *To live is to listen to the message of life itself. If I were called upon to state in few words the essence of everything I was trying to say both as an author and as a preacher, it would be something like this: Listen to your life. See it for the fathomless mystery it is. In the boredom and pain of it no less than in the excitement and gladness: touch, taste, smell your way to the holy and hidden heart of it because in the last analysis all moments are key moments, and life itself is grace.* [5]

My second child, Jasmine, is an affectionate girl. While she is engaged in activity, scurrying through the house on her way to who knows where, she will momentarily put her arms around me, squeeze hard, and then run off. She is living and loving. She is doing and feeling. She is aware of herself and her needs as well as aware of me and mine. I'm learning from her ability to be engaged fully and openly in the unfolding moment.

To live on the surface of things and to not listen to what our own hearts are telling us is to deny God's calling on our lives.

The Danish philosopher Soren Kierkegaard suggests in *Purity of Heart* that to live unintentionally is to be spiritually negligent.

> *At each man's birth there comes into being an eternal vocation for him, expressly for him. To be true to himself in relation to this eternal vocation is the highest thing a man can practice, and as that most profound poet has said: "Self-love is not so vile a sin as self-neglect."* [6]

WE ARE ASKED TO THOROUGHLY IDENTIFY WITH OUR OWN COMMUNITIES

When Jesus asked Peter to "feed my sheep," he was doing more than assigning an important task. Jesus was suggesting that if Peter were to really live a life of love, he must identify more faithfully with his own community. He must join them. He must take more responsibility for their welfare. He must serve them. He must belong to them.

"Feed my sheep," is a call to offer oneself to God's people with open hands and open heart. It is a summons to identify with our spiritual family and all of the imperfections and pain that go along with it. It is a call to embrace one's community and not to compete with it.

Peter has prided himself on his fierce loyalty to Jesus. His commitment has been defined in comparison to what others did or did not do, however. After he denies Christ to the insistent woman in Caiphas' courtyard the night Jesus is crucified, he persists, later on, in competing with the disciple John: *"And what about him, Lord?"* Even in failure, Peter seeks to justify himself by comparing himself to his rival.

Jesus points out to Peter that his relationship with him is defined to a great extent by his (Peter's) relationship with everyone else. As Peter is able to truly join his own community, he is able to fully join and identify with Christ.

This may sound strange, but a turning point in my life came when I decided to join my own church!

ONE STEP REMOVED

This may sound strange, but a turning point in my life

came when I decided to join my own church. I don't mean join it "officially," but join it emotionally. I realized that I was standing on the outside looking in. I was comfortable being "the leader" or "the professional," but had not identified with the church as a person, as a fellow sojourner. I was safe hiding behind my roles and responsibilities, but I could not genuinely bring healing to others or experience healing myself when I was always one step removed from them.

On the night Jesus predicted Peter's betrayal, Jesus offers to wash Peter's feet and Peter initially refuses it. Somehow Peter knew that to allow Jesus to serve him in this way would eventuate in an irreconcilable dilemma. Peter was not ready to offer himself to his friends and therefore he could not participate in Jesus' offer of service to him. He could not freely receive because he could not freely give. He could not give because he could not reconcile himself to being an equal with his brothers. He was on the outside looking in.

My first few years as pastor of what was then a very small church were pure honeymoon. I loved preaching and teaching. Our congregation was delighted to simply have survived as a new church and everything we did together was novel and exciting.

After a few years, the honeymoon began to wear off. Not everyone in the church thought I was the best pastor they had ever encountered. I was challenged by conflict that arose over the direction and style of the church. I was shocked that not everyone agreed with me on everything. I did not handle disagreement and dissension skillfully. People left the church and some of the people that stayed didn't seem very happy.

I didn't consciously decide that I was going to close my heart to the people in my congregation. I didn't wake up one day and say to myself, "I'm not going to trust anyone again. I'm just going to try to be a 'good professional' pastor and do the job without making myself too vulnerable."

I didn't say these words explicitly to myself, but over a period of time I slipped into an approach to leadership characterized by this attitude. I want to clarify that I do believe we can learn valuable lessons about how to be "wise as serpents and innocent as doves." It is wise to learn how to be circumspect about how vulnerable we are to certain people. My problem was that I was overreacting to being hurt. I had pulled my heart out of my own community. I was living on the periphery of my God-given circle of fellowship. I was taking a cowardly and easy way around the difficult assignment of living in spiritual accountability.

During this time of self-imposed emotional isolation, I read Dietrich Bonhoeffer's book *Life Together.* I came upon a passage that struck me so hard I felt as if I had been body-slammed to the ground:

A pastor should not complain about his congregation, certainly never to other people, but also not to God. A congregation has not been entrusted to him in order that he should become its accuser before God and men. When a person becomes alienated from a Christian community in which he has been placed and begins to complain about it, he had better examine himself first to see whether the trouble is not due to his "wish dream" that should be shattered by God; and if this be the case, let him thank God for leading him into this predicament.[7]

When I read this I had not been complaining about my congregation, but I certainly was feeling disappointed over them. Bonhoeffer's phrase "wish dream" struck me as relevant. I was feeling disillusioned because my community was not living up to my expectations. The problem, I could now see, was that I had not fully appreciated the real meaning of community. It was not about servicing my needs; it was not about idealized experiences together; it was not about relational nirvana. It is about giving and receiving love and this process is rarely glossy and smooth.

African church leader Kefa Sempangi expresses the heart of this issue as clearly and unflinchingly as I have ever heard it:

Hardly any of us can go to our own Christian community and say: "This is my body which is broken for you. I am laying all my professional skills, abilities, and economic resources at your disposal. Take them and use them as you see fit." We cannot say this because we are not broken. We are too proud to give our lives away to people who are not perfect. We don't want to lose ourselves for sinners. We want to find the perfect person and the perfect community, but we never find them. So, like Judas, we make only a partial commitment to the body of believers to which we belong, and we find our identity in our rebellion from them.[8]

Our healing is inseparable from our participation in the restoration of others.

Jesus forgives Peter unconditionally. His love is not manipulatively withdrawn. Jesus does not play games with Peter's emotions or maneuver him. There is no doubt, not a sliver of uncertainty in my mind (and I think in Peter's) that Jesus did not wholeheartedly accept Peter back into the fold. The "difficult conversation" that Jesus has with Peter was not about Peter atoning for his failure; it was about Peter seeing and addressing his true spiritual condition. It was about getting to the real issues as to why he had failed in the first place. It was about how to prepare Peter for his best possible future.

And so Jesus does not hand Peter a cheap or easy way out.

Our spiritual health and healing is very much connected with our willingness to get up off the floor and begin to offer ourselves to people again. No one who is leading and serving others is exempt from the heart-wrenching struggle against one's own instincts of self-preservation. To heal oneself by healing others is a counterintuitive undertaking. It is an act of spiritual discernment and intentional love. It demonstrates an innate grasp for what Jesus has done for us.

When I was a pastor, every few months we scheduled a healing service. We asked people who are "brokenhearted or bruised" to come and allow members of our prayer teams to lay hands on them and pray a simple prayer of healing for them.

During one of these meetings, a small woman sought me out. I normally don't pray for people in these meetings myself, but help to match people and their needs with trained prayer teams. I do this so people are not depending on the minister (me) but on the strength and resources of the community. She obviously wanted me to pray for her as she was avoiding the prayer team and seeking me out with eagle eyes.

When she found me she got straight to the point: "I want to be healed from wounds I have from pastors who have abused me."

My first thought was, "Oh boy, here we go." I did not know this woman and it was obvious that she was trying to manipulate me or "set me up" to feel obliged to her in some way. I had seen this kind of thing before. So I prayed a standard prayer and hoped to be free of this needy and perhaps manipulative person.

After I prayed my tidy prayer, she looked at me (and through me!) and said, "I'm not trying to curry favor or sympathy from you Pastor Sam, I'm really trying to create a path back into the church." I spent the next twenty minutes listening to her story. I was moved by her sincerity and realized that I had read her wrong and had jumped to conclusions. I prayed with her again and hugged her. I also apologized to her for being initially dismissive toward her. She was very gracious and forgave me. I felt that we had connected and I had been able to recover from a potential foul-up.

Later that week I made this entry in my journal: "Today I realized that the wounds that 'Betty' (not her real name) incurred by her pastor are wounds that I have perpetrated, albeit unintentionally, on members of my congregation. I am in need of healing and restoration as much or more than she is. In fact, I needed to pray for her to heal my own wounds perhaps more than she needed prayer for herself. Thank you for sending her. And forgive me."

Sometimes it hurts to get healed. It hurts to roll up our sleeves, take off our shoes and wade into the pain of other people's lives. In almost every instance where I am called upon by God to exercise compassion and empathy towards someone, there is a place of wounding in me that needs healing as well. The Psalmist asks God to search out the ways of pain that reside within us:

"Search me, O God, and know my heart;

Try me and know my anxious thoughts;

And see if there be any hurtful way in me..."

—Psalm 139: 23-24

Annie Dillard eloquently describes what it means to delve into the depths of human pain and unearth healing:

In the deeps are the violence and terror of which psychology has warned us. But if you ride these monsters down, if you drop with them farther over the world's rim, you find what our sciences cannot locate or name, the substrate, the ocean or matrix or ether which buoys the rest, which gives goodness its power for good, and evil its power for evil, the unified field: our complex and inexplicable caring for each other, and for our life together here. This is given. It is not learned.[9]

Jesus beckons Peter to heal his own wounds by nourishing his spiritual flock. Decades after Jesus' and Peter's conversation at the Sea of Galilee, an aged Peter writes to the Christian churches: "Shepherd the flock of God which is among you...willingly." I imagine that these words now have multiple layers of meaning and significance to Peter. He has been personally healed and restored by employing his vocation. He has "fed the sheep" and thereby been supplied. ⌇

personal response

1. On a scale from 1-10, how "fully awake" do you sense you are in regards to your ministry and family? Explain.

2. Can you recall times in your life and ministry after a failure when you were quick to justify yourself by comparing yourself to a rival? Explain.

3. What will it take for you to begin being "in touch" and living "intentionally?"

change

Until your level of dissatisfaction outweighs your fear of failure, things in your life will rarely really change .
–Sam Rockwell

Facing Your True Self
From Barrenness to Fruitfulness

Hannah, why do you weep? Why do you not eat?
And why is your heart grieved
—I Samuel 1:8

*D*o you ever feel your life is under construction?

A while back, while I was processing the prospect of accepting a new ministry role, the gym that I frequent was doing work in the parking lot. They had orange construction cones everywhere and my normal parking spot was not available. Every day for a month I parked in a different place and I could never remember after a workout where I had parked. I wandered aimlessly in the parking lot, wondering if I had lost my car or my mind.

Some of us may be feeling a bit displaced in the transitions that come with our life.

I want to walk you through a text and a process that for me is not just a teaching, but the most palatable experience of my life.

This story is about finding our way through a personal transformation.   It's about identifying the signposts along the way that take us from barrenness to fruitfulness. Recognizing these markers does not make the journey easy, but it helps us to know where we are on the map and to navigate our way forward with more confidence and hope.

Now there was a certain man of Ramathaim Zophim, of the mountains of Ephraim, and his name was Elkanah the son of Jeroham, the son of Elihu,[a] the son of Tohu, the son of Zuph, an Ephraimite. And he had two wives: the name of one was Hannah, and the name of the other Peninnah. Peninnah had children, but Hannah had no children. This man went up from his city yearly to worship and sacrifice to the LORD of hosts in Shiloh. Also the two sons of Eli, Hophni and Phinehas, the priests of the LORD, were there. And whenever the time came for Elkanah to make an offering, he would give portions to Peninnah his wife and to all her sons and daughters. But to Hannah he would give a double portion, for he loved Hannah, although the LORD had closed her womb. And her rival also provoked her severely, to make her miserable, because the

LORD had closed her womb. So it was, year by year, when she went up to the house of the LORD, that she provoked her; therefore she wept and did not eat.

Then Elkanah her husband said to her, "Hannah, why do you weep? Why do you not eat? And why is your heart grieved? Am I not better to you than ten sons?"

So Hannah arose after they had finished eating and drinking in Shiloh. Now Eli the priest was sitting on the seat by the doorpost of the tabernacle of the LORD. And she was in bitterness of soul, and prayed to the LORD and wept in anguish. Then she made a vow and said, "O LORD of hosts, if You will indeed look on the affliction of Your maidservant and remember me, and not forget Your maidservant, but will give Your maidservant a male child, then I will give him to the LORD all the days of his life, and no razor shall come upon his head."

And it happened, as she continued praying before the LORD, that Eli watched her mouth. Now Hannah spoke in her heart; only her lips moved, but her voice was not heard. Therefore Eli thought she was drunk. So Eli said to her, "How long will you be drunk? Put your wine away from you!"

But Hannah answered and said, "No, my lord, I am a woman of sorrowful spirit. I have drunk neither wine nor intoxicating drink, but have poured out my soul before the LORD.

Do not consider your maidservant a wicked woman, for out of the abundance of my complaint and grief I have spoken until now."

Then Eli answered and said, "Go in peace, and the God of Israel grant your petition which you have asked of Him."

And she said, "Let your maidservant find favor in your sight." So the woman went her way and ate, and her face was no longer sad. —1 Samuel 1

The story of Hannah is about a woman who couldn't have a baby and then could.

If you scratch just a bit below the surface you discover much more. It describes a process one enters into when one is emerging from a place of barrenness or wilderness or plateau. Whether it is your marriage, your money, your ministry or whatever, I hope you can locate yourself on the road-map provided and find your bearings. There are several landmarks in this journey that are universal elements in the personal journey of transformation – they form the emotional and spiritual sub-text of Hannah's story and of ours.

This is the story of a woman who had lived with an unfulfilled need until the longing became so intense she couldn't live with it anymore.

Verse 9 provides the turning point in Hannah's life: "So Hannah arose."

She has been in this place many times before but this time she was asked to name her dissatisfaction and the cause of her unhappiness. She was asked to account for it. We don't know how the conversation unfolded between Elkanah and Hannah after that. But it is clear that in the process of naming and accounting for her grief, something catalytic took place in Hannah and she took the first steps of responsibility for her discontent. She took "ownership" of that longing and the dissatisfaction rather than continuing to be victimized by it. So on this particular day, prompted by the burning question "Why do you weep and why is your heart grieved?" Hannah finally stands up, takes action and nothing is the same again.

DISCERN THE GIFT OF DISSATISFACTION

Can the experience of dissatisfaction ever really be a "gift'? If I am commanded to "give thanks in all circumstances; for this is the will of God in Christ Jesus for you" (1 Thes. 5:18) how is it possible for dissatisfaction to ever be anything good?

It can be something good – a gift - when it is a prompt from God moving us to step beyond what is known and out into His greater purposes for us. Dissatisfaction may be the key to unlock both our physical and emotional energy and inform our depth of insight. Dissatisfaction becomes a holy prompt when it moves us out of our self-defined comfort zone into the larger expanses of God's great vision for us, as individuals or as a people.

At what point can we tell when the dissatisfaction in our life is really a God-prompt and not just ungratefulness or selfishness? For most of us it is when the pain of the dissatisfaction becomes unbearable, like it did for Hannah. At this point pain can become the life-giving prompt to make changes necessary for our fulfillment.

Three elements must coalesce to make a positive change in your life:

- Energy

Until the desire for change tips the scale, we remain unhappily content.

- Insight

- Dissatisfaction

We all know we need energy and insight. These are the two positive elements that we are always trying to augment. But change does not occur until all three of these factors are present. (Any two of them without a third is incomplete.)

E + I − D = status quo maintained

E + D − I = frantic activity without change

I + D − E = complainer

It is easy to mistake dissatisfaction for selfishness or ingratitude. It is, after all, the negative element of the three. BUT IT IS A GIFT FROM GOD.

Ironically, dissatisfaction may be the key to unlock both our physical and emotional energy and inform our insight. All three elements are present in this passage from Deuteronomy:

> *He found him in a desert land*
> *And in the wasteland, a howling wilderness;*
> *He encircled him, He instructed him,*
> *He kept him as the apple of His eye.*
> *As an eagle stirs up its nest,*
> *Hovers over its young,*

Spreading out its wings, taking them up,

Carrying them on its wings. —Deuteronomy 32: 10-11

In a state of "holy discontent" that is prompted by God to get us to take the next steps in growth or advancement – God is the mother eagle removing the down feathers from the nest (removing our comfort props) and urging us out of the nest to fly.

Why do we wait so often to deal with dissatisfaction until it becomes unbearable pain? Feelings of dissatisfaction reside right next to the unarticulated "payoffs" for staying where we are. Until the desire for change tips the scale, we are unhappily content.

Hannah enjoyed the sympathy of her husband and the favored place in the home. Perhaps she thought this would be enough. Perhaps she thought this was all that she could have.

It takes some courage to ask what are your payoffs for things to remain the way they are? What benefits do you gain by not rocking the boat of your circumstances? There are usually payoffs that keep us from risking change, but the dreams God plants in us and His promises for them remain a holy provocateur.

God's promises stir up expectation and sometimes spiritual discontentment.

To Abram: *Then He brought him outside and said, "Look now toward heaven, and count the stars if you are able to number them."*

And He said to him, 'So shall your descendants be.'" —Genesis 15:5

To Moses: *"Come now, and I will send you to Pharaoh that you may bring My people, the children of Israel, out of Egypt."*
—Exodus 3:10

To Joseph: *Now Joseph had a dream, and he told it to his brothers; and they hated him even more.* —Genesis 37:5

DISCERNING YOUR DISSATISFACTION

Make a point to look at what you are dissatisfied with in your own life and take some steps to sharpen your focus.

- Get away from the grind. Reflect and make lists and ask hard questions.

- Identify your payoffs. Any situation you stay in has its payoffs; that's why you don't change. Either quit complaining or admit you like things the way they are.

- Admit your fears. Your fears are a treasure of information if you will explore them.

- Of whom are you jealous? (Jealousy is a nasty emotion that can teach us a lot. It's the back door of desire. What we won't admit we want will come back to bite us through envy. What is it telling you?)

- Face your sorrows. Name them before God, write them out and release them to Him. Ignoring real pain can carry some terrible costs, to ourselves as to others.

DISCERN THE VOICE OF THE CRITIC

Looking at the story of Hannah and the road map it gives us we can identify a series of landmarks.

First landmark: you're dissatisfied

Second landmark: you have a critic

> *And her rival also provoked her severely, to make her miserable, because the LORD had closed her womb. So it was, year by year, when she went up to the house of the LORD, that she provoked her; therefore she wept and did not eat.*
> —*1 Samuel 1:6*

A nemesis serves an important purpose: he/she is a mirror of the lies you believe. In this case, Peninnah "blesses" Hannah by forcing her to deal with her beliefs about herself and God.

When Hannah distinguishes her own voice from her critic's voice, and the critic's voice from God's voice, Peninnah drops out of the story. Later Hannah sings: *"I smile at my enemies."*

Most of the battle with the inner dialogue is simply the process of seeing what we think, getting it out in front of us. The lies and truth of our inner critic or inner spirit is fairly obvious. Lies are not that difficult to detect once their camouflage is revealed. Try it and see what you think!

HANNAH IS LIVING WITH A SET OF LIES THAT HAVE BECOME "HERS"

- I'm lucky to have what little I have and I might lose it if I ask for more.

- Whatever I do, I must do perfectly.

- I don't get my hopes up.

- I keep my head down to avoid enemy fire.

If we don't communicate well while we are in transition, our relationships will become such a distraction that we will get stuck in the transition.

- I plan for worst-case scenario.

- I don't ask for what I want.

- I plan to be the expendable one.

- I don't deserve to have what I want.

- I have unforgivable and fatal flaws.

- I deserve the negative people in my life and can't do anything about them. (You are the organizing principle for all the people in your life. Look at your facebook page! It is a huge indicator.)

OKAY, YOU'VE OWNED IT, NOW DISOWN IT

Do you know the sound of your own voice? Do you recognize the voice that is the real and authentic you and not the fabrication of other people's beliefs and perceptions of you?

- Get a disciplined listener – someone you can trust and respect.

- Exercise the courage to say what you think without editing it for what you think someone else will hear. Listen to what is really there in your thoughts.

- Keep a stream of consciousness journal.

- The answer is not reciting empty affirmations to yourself: "I'm good enough and smart enough, and doggone it people like me," but simply identifying a lie when it is present.

- *"A curse without a cause will not alight."* If you know and can affirm what is real and true, the lies lose their power to influence or hurt you.

- Jesus said the "accuser has nothing in me." If you know the truth, the truth does set you free!

- Lies are harmless unless they "synchronize" in you. They can do nothing until we believe and act on them.

BE CLEAR WITH OTHERS

- First landmark: you're dissatisfied

- Second landmark: you have a critic

- Third landmark: you're misunderstood

YOUR CRITICS ARE ONE THING
YOUR FRIENDS ARE ANOTHER

If we don't communicate well while we are in transition,

our relationships will become such a distraction that we will get stuck in the transition and probably do more damage while we are there.

If you are changing or processing a transition, the people in your life need turn signals. When you are doing the turning, it's your responsibility to do the signaling.

When we are changing, (exchanging what we have been for something new) , the people closest to us are left to interpret our change, often without much help from us. This takes the focus off the change and on to the relationship. This is normal and part of the process.

There are two very typical ways that Hannah is misunderstood by those in her set of relationships:

- "What's wrong with me?" (Elkanah) This is the reaction that takes your change personally.

- "This is temporary inebriation!" (Eli) This is the reaction that does not take your change seriously.

PITFALLS

- Blame: "I'm unhappy because of you."

- Withdrawal: "I'll go on without you."

- Threat: "I'll leave unless you change."

- Arrogance: "Figure it out on your own."

Hannah offers a textbook response of humility and clarity.

> *"No, my lord, I am a woman of sorrowful spirit. I have drunk neither wine nor intoxicating drink, but have poured out my soul before the LORD. Do not consider your maidservant a wicked woman, for out of the abundance of my complaint and grief I have spoken until now."*   —*I Samuel 1:15-16*

HANNAH'S RESPONSE TO BEING MISUNDERSTOOD

- She addresses her accuser with respect.

- She truthfully identifies herself.

- She expresses her emotion without blaming: "I'm in pain."

- She meekly and clearly corrects the misunderstanding by stating the facts: "I have not been drinking."

- She takes complete responsibility for herself: "I have an issue with God, not with you."

- She appeals to his patience and understanding: "I'm in pain."

BE CLEAR WITH GOD

- First landmark: you're dissatisfied: (learn to discern your dissatisfaction)

- Second landmark: you have a critic: (learn to recognize the voice of the critic)

- Third landmark: you're misunderstood: (learn to use turn signals)

- Fourth landmark: you don't know what you want

Often what we want has a redemptive dimension to it, beyond the initial potentially selfish motivation. Hannah wanted a baby for her own sense of worth and significance, God wanted Samuel to be His spokesperson, a prophet to the nation.

The articulation of her prayer is underscored by repetition in the text: "Eli watched her lips move...her lips moved."

My point is not that God will give you what you want. My point is that you have to start with what you know, you have to face it, own it, put it out there to Him. This is the raw material God uses. He expects you to be a spiritual adult not a petulant child who expects everyone to read your mind and anticipate your needs. This is also the building block of intimacy with Him. Tell Him the truth about who you are. What you long for most is the surest litmus test to your authentic self. It isn't a surprise to

God, but it may come as that to you.

The cost of not living authentically and denying life to the dreams God has already planted in you will adversely affect not only you but everyone around you as well. The longing that cannot be denied will impact and influence every one of your relationships with its presence.

> *Nothing has a stronger influence psychologically on their environment and especially on their children than the unlived life of the parent.* – C. G. Jung

Use these practices as a way to articulate your desires to God. I'm not saying you'll get everything on your list but it will certainly give you some insight into patterns in yourself and maybe clear out some of the clutter in your thoughts by putting them down on paper!

- Make a list of a hundred things you want

- Describe three alternative lives you could live

- Make a bucket list

False humility is just a disguise for pride. Humility becomes genuine in us when we do the hard work of wrestling with God and emerging from the struggle with a sense of destiny and calling that NO ONE can take away from us. We are able to stand up and say: 'This is who I am and what I am called to be and do."

God requires this kind of confidence from us. When Jesus emerged from 40 days in the wilderness he stood before the synagogue and declared, "This is who I Am." When He was confronted with Judas and His betrayers after Gethsemane He declared,

"Ego ami." "I AM."

How are you defining yourself in the face of adversity?

CONCLUSION

This is not about getting what you want. It is about God getting what He wants, you receiving from God and then offering back to Him what He has given. It is an inward and outbound journey.

If there are orange cones signaling change in your life,

- Discern the gift of dissatisfaction

- Discern the voice of the critic

- Be clear with others

- Be clear with God

> "Go in peace, and the God of Israel grant your petition which you have asked of Him." And she said, "Let your maidservant find favor in your sight." So the woman went her way and ate, and her face was no longer sad. —1 Samuel 1:17-18

My prayer focus for you is a bold one:

Lord grant our requests and give us favor.

personal response

1. Describe where you sense you are in the Energy, Insight and Dissatisfaction mix.

2. In what areas of your life are you unhappily content? Explain.

3. In the present, when you are misunderstood, what is your normal or habitual reaction to those not understanding you?

fortitude

You must do the thing you cannot do..
–Eleanor Roosevelt

Confronting Your Worst Fears

Confidently Answering Your Call

I promise you what I promised Moses: 'Wherever you set foot, you will be on land I have given you ... No one will be able to stand against you as long as you live. For I will be with you as I was with Moses. I will not fail you or abandon you. —Joshua 1:1-3, NLT

*M*oses' life changed forever as the result of a simple God-ordered tactic; a flame in the desert. Moses was so accustomed to his settled routine that God devised a creative means to get his attention.

Now Moses was tending the flock of Jethro his father-in-law, the priest of Midian. And he led the flock to the back of the desert, and came to Horeb, the mountain of God. And the Angel of the Lord appeared to him in a flame of fire from the midst of a bush. So he looked and behold, the bush was burning with fire, but the bush was not consumed.

Then Moses said, "I will now turn aside and see this great sight, why the bush does not burn." So when the Lord saw that he turned aside to look, God called to him from the midst of the bush and said, "Moses, Moses!" And he said, "Here I am." Then He said, "Do not draw near this place. Take your sandals off your feet, for the place you stand is holy ground." Moreover He said, "I am the God of your father– the God of Abraham, the God of Isaac, and the God of Jacob." And Moses hid his face, for he was afraid to look upon God.

And the Lord said, "I have surely seen the oppression of My people who are in Egypt, and have heard their cry because of their taskmasters, for I know their sorrows. So I have come down to deliver them out of the hand of the Egyptians and to bring them up from that land to a good and large land to a land flowing with milk and honey, to the place of the Canaanites, and the Hittites, and the Amorites and the Perizzites and the Hivites and the Jebusites. Now therefore, behold, the cry of the children of Israel has come to Me, and I have also seen the oppression with which the Egyptians oppress them; Come now, therefore, and I will send you to

Pharaoh, that you may bring My people, the children of Israel, out of Egypt."

But Moses said to God, "Who am I that I should go to Pharaoh, and that I should bring the children of Israel out of Egypt?"

So He said, "I will certainly be with you..."

—*Exodus 3: 1-12*

THE HOLY GROUND OF CHANGE

Moses has been ensconced in a forty-year-old routine. He has long since resigned himself to the fact that his life has become defined by lesser ideals than his youthful days in Pharaoh's court. He had been raised and educated to think of himself as a leader. He had even entertained dreams of being a deliverer. His heart had once stirred passionately with grief, love, and compassion for his people and their plight.

As an Israelite raised by the daughter of Pharaoh in the grand and exalted palace, he had watched his own people suffer as slaves under the tyranny of the Egyptians. He had probably been taught to believe that he was special, that destiny had touched his life with a great purpose. As an infant, he had been miraculously and dramatically rescued from death. His early life experience had led him to see himself as a favored and exceptional son. It seemed that God had put His hand upon him.

But that had all changed.

Forty years is enough time for reality to become paramount – even in the toughest and greatest minds. It's enough time to learn to appreciate the simple pleasures of maintaining a family business and enjoying a predictable, and peaceful existence. After four decades, the concerns of Moses' youth had been slowly replaced with a sense of relinquishment – the overwhelming difficulties of his people would have to be tackled by someone else.

Moses had undergone

Moses was not looking for burning bushes. He was content with his life as it was. He couldn't hear God until he stepped away from his familiar path.

some necessary losses in the wilderness. He had surrendered the notion that he could single-handedly secure the release of his fellow Israelites by sheer will and determination. He was more realistic, perhaps disillusioned, regarding his role in the larger scope of things. Before his exile, he had failed to protect even one poor, abused Israelite successfully, and in the process had been misunderstood and vilified by his brethren.

He was happy to take care of his father-in-law's sheep. Sheep didn't talk back, shake fists at him, or question his motives.

TURNING ASIDE

Moses' life changed forever as the result of a simple God-ordered tactic – a flame in the desert. Moses was so accustomed to his settled routine that God devised a creative means to get his attention. In the text, the phrase "turned aside" is used twice in the space of two sentences. Moses, it appears, had to coach himself away from his well-worn treadmill: "I will now turn aside." He pinched himself. He called himself to attention. Moses was not looking for burning bushes. He was content with his life as it was. He couldn't hear God until he stepped away from his familiar path. Feed the sheep. Watch the sheep. Water the sheep. Shear the sheep. Walk. Eat. Sleep.

Walk. Eat. Sleep. Walk. Burning bush!

Odd circumstances serve as the platform from which God speaks.

Transitions often take us by surprise. The situation that has our attention may have a message for us – "Get out of your rut and pay attention! Your feet are on holy ground!" This day in the life of Moses had started out as any other normal day but his life's journey had just taken an unalterable turn.

SEEING YOUR BURNING BUSH

The ability to recognize burning bushes may require insight. Life can often seem random and arbitrary. God-orchestrated circumstances can appear like those holographic picture-puzzles, which at first glance look like pure chaos. But if one can see "into" the picture, see beyond the haphazard blizzard of shapes and colors, one can see a full-bodied image – meaning and order – emerging from amidst the muddle. This is how God's voice is sometimes discerned.

New sets of realities, however, may require some self-directed coaching, just as Moses said to himself, "I will now turn aside and see this great sight." To be open to God may dictate that we place our lives in God's frame of reference by saying to ourselves: "I'm going to change my direction and pay attention to what God is saying to me – My circumstances are directed by God, – even though everything seems so senseless and confused. Therefore, I will not surrender to self-pity or despair.   God is at work."

WHO AM I?

Although Moses had forgotten his dream, God had not forgotten Moses. At the burning bush, God gave Moses a quick primer of the history of the Israelites. Moses knew the story, but no longer felt the drive to be personally involved. As Moses stood and listened to God rehearse the dire state of affairs of His people, a feeling of dread descended upon him. He was being called upon! Just when he had come to peace with his life, God wanted him to be a hero!

Moses was being called upon to return to the site of a shameful act in his life; He had killed an Egyptian who was abusing an Israelite slave. Moses must now address his own past and failures.

He was being called upon to lead people who, at last contact, had slandered and rejected him. His command was to provide leadership to people who did not appreciate him.

He was being called upon to personally confront one of the

most vicious and cruel tyrants in history – go head-to-head with a brutal enemy.

These are the three challenges we all face, no matter what our particular assignment may be:

- **Face Your Failures**: Return to the site of your greatest shame.

- **Face Your Enemy**: Eye-to-eye, head-to-head, toe-to-toe.

- **Face Your Followers**: Lead people who may have already rejected you once.

Does this sound familiar to anyone?

It wasn't just the overwhelming external realities that terrified him. He had a host of internal ghosts and fears to face as well.

Moses had been abandoned, of necessity, by his mother.

He had been sent down the Nile River as a baby to escape the genocidal "tendencies" of another Pharaoh a generation earlier. Raised by a surrogate mother, he had never fully realized his own identity. Separated from his mother and rejected by his people, Moses' deepest and truest question was not, "Who am I?" but "Will you abandon me?"

Whenever we are challenged with a new assignment or a new set of obstacles, it is natural to take stock of our capacities and ask ourselves, "Am I up to this?" But God goes to the very heart of Moses' doubts and fears. He doesn't seem to answer the question Moses asks. He seems to ignore it altogether. It is because the question doesn't accurately reflect the real issues in Moses' life. God answers with what seems to be a non sequitur: "I will certainly be with you."

"I will certainly be with you" does not answer the question Moses asked, but it does answer his most important question, "Will You abandon me?"

I WILL CERTAINLY BE WITH YOU

If we are to meet the challenges of facing our enemies, addressing the past squarely, and exercising leadership where it may not always be appreciated, it will require a new definition of personal security.

Our security must go bone deep.

Our security must reach beyond the superficial props of success, money, and accomplishment and go to the core of who we are. We must know that the presence of God goes with us. We must know that there is a reserve of strength and confidence that transcends our own previously defined capabilities. The statement, "I will certainly be with you," cuts to the bone. It touches on the nerve of our existence. It answers all the questions, really, that can be asked.

The question, "Who am I?" is a legitimate one. It's important to know oneself, to appreciate one's own frame. Ultimately, however, the answer to this question, whatever it may be, is an inadequate gauge for determining God's best for our lives. It is a question that can never be answered to our satisfaction.

Self-discovery can be like peeling the layers of an onion in search of the onion. There is no "there-it-is!" Perpetual introspection leads to despair and a sense of futility. We are, ultimately, what we do. The road to self-discovery is the road to whomever it is that God is calling us to become. Self-discovery must focus on the future, primarily, and on the past, secondarily. The only way we can risk taking new steps of faith to get to a new place is to have our personal security rooted, not in superficial self-definitions ("I can do anything!"), but in the knowledge that God's presence is the ultimate starting point for each new risk in life.

"Who am I?"

"I will certainly be with you."

This exchange beautifully captures the most important factor involved in embarking upon a new assignment. The necessary courage and resources for change are not often present in our emotional arsenal. We must step into the unknown based on a presence and power greater than ourselves.

And God knows this. This is why He doesn't waste time attempting to answer Moses' question with superficial information. "Moses you have been educated in fine schools, you are energetic and resourceful, you are talented and gifted." No, Moses is left with the one truth that really matters: "I am enough."

Several years ago, when I was a pastor, my church experienced a church split. I remember a moment that

If we are to meet the challenges of facing our enemies, addressing the past squarely, and exercising leadership where it may not always be appreciated, it will require a new definition of personal security.

will always represent a turning point in my life. Only a few weeks after the turmoil of the split, I was standing in the back of the church sanctuary during the worship and music time. I was trying to control the sense of dread and hurt that I felt. I was trying to muster the strength to get through the service without falling apart. This church that used to hold so much hope and joy for me was now the last place in the world I wanted to be. I felt that people whom I loved and trusted had rejected me. I felt abandoned and betrayed. I felt utterly inadequate to lead or inspire the people who were still left.

"Lord," I whispered, "I can't stay here. Give me one good reason why I shouldn't leave and get on with my life somewhere else."

I can't explain how I know He spoke to me, but the answer I received in that moment has guided my ministry for many years: "I'll be with you."

This was not the answer I was looking for, but it was the most sufficient assurance I could have received for the challenges that lay ahead. ⌫

personal response

1. When caught off-guard by the manifestation of a burning bush, how do you face your fears? Explain.

2. As Moses was called upon to return to the place of his shameful murder of the Egyptian, what thoughts and/or emotions race through your heart and mind when thinking how God may do the same with you? Explain.

3. As you realize that you have some fears due to the lack of personal security, what steps will you start taking immediately to begin building the confidence that will carry you through?

....

....

....

....

....

....

....

....

being clear

To be nobody but yourself

in a world which is doing its best

to make you everybody else,

means to fight the hardest battle

which any human being can fight and

never stop fighting.

—e.e. cummings

Identifying Your Own Voice

Leading with Confidence and Integrity

I promise you what I promised Moses: 'Wherever you set foot, you will

be on land I have given you ... No one will be able to stand against you

as long as you live. For I will be with you as I was with Moses. I will

not fail you or abandon you. –Joshua 1:1-3, NLT

*P*astoral authority is like a heavy-duty power tool. In skill-ful hands it can make one more efficient and more fruitful, but misused by the inept it can prove extremely hazardous or even deadly. To lead our churches effectively demands that we be nei-ther heavy-handed on overusing our power, nor wishy-washy through fear of using it at all. A balanced approach to spiritu-al authority pivots on our ability as leaders to define ourselves clearly and to take unambiguously defined positions in the face of confusion and resistance. Church life, as we all know from costly experience, abounds with conflicts centering on this issue.

For instance, every experienced pastor I have ever met has his own tale of a "Jezebel" encounter. We all know how it gets started. Someone in the congregation begins to challenge the direction the church is going or to question the pastor's credibility by subtle comments ("I sure hope the pastor is hearing the Lord on this"), empathetic "understanding" ("I'm sure the pastor means to be sensitive to our feelings"), or superior spiritual insight ("The Lord spoke to me and told me..."). It is amusing to catalogue the number of places where leaders have declared their particular geographical location a haven for the "Jezebel spirit." The problem arises from two factors: the invasiveness of a strong personality from the congregation and the commensurate passivity or 'tolerance' of the pastor (Revelation 2:20). Both conditions must be present for a "Jezebel" situation to develop and cause damage.

Just as common, though, are the myriad of horror stories from laymen – those who still attend church, those who drift from this church to that, or those who have given up on churches altogether – of the brow-beating, domineering pastor whose control over his flock is absolute. These tales run amazingly parallel to one another, as do the "Jezebel" chronicles. There is no denying, of course, that there exist pastors who are so insensitive to others and so insecure in themselves that their control of everything that occurs in the church may not be questioned. This problem also thrives only under dual conditions: the passivity and dependence of the followers and the concomitant overpowering personality of the leader.

I am convinced that both these common church diseases can be cured – or avoided altogether. The answer lies in a reorientation of the pastor himself. An effective leader must steer carefully between two errors: "The true church consists of its parishioners and I am but their servant," and "This is my church and I must govern it." Rather, a pastor must learn to lead from a deep sense of who he is and where he is headed as a person.

SELF-DIFFERENTIATION

Edwin Friedman, in his book, *Generation to Generation: Family Process in Church and Synagogue* writes about the importance of a spiritual leader's "self-differentiation".

> **Differentiation** *simply means: the capacity to become one-self out of one's self with minimum reactivity to the positions or reactivity of others. Differentiation is charting one's own way by means of one's own internal guidance system, rather*

——————— ❦ ———————

An effective leader must steer carefully between two errors: 1. The true church consists of its parishioners and I am but their servant, and 2. This is my church and I must govern it.

than perpetually eying the scope to see where others are.

Differentiation refers more to a process than to a goal that can ever be achieved. (To say, "I 'differentiated' from my wife, my child, my parent," etc., proves that the speaker does not understand the concept.) It refers to a direction in life rather than a state of being, to the capacity to take a stand in an intense emotional system, to saying "I" when others are demanding "we" to containing one's reactivity to the activity of others (which includes the ability to avoid being polarized), to maintaining a non-anxious presence in the face of anxious others. It refers, as well, to knowing where one ends and another begins, to be able to cease automatically being one of the systems emotional dominoes, to being clear

about ones own personal values and goals, to taking maxi-
mum responsibility for ones own emotional being and destiny
rather than blaming others or the context: culture, gender, or
environmental forces. It is an emotional concept, not a cere-
bral one, but it does require clearheadedness. And it has enor-
mous consequence for new ways of thinking about leadership.
But it is a lifetime project with no one ever getting more than
seventy percent of the way to the goal.[10]

Differentiation is not to be equated, however, with simi-
lar-sounding ideas such as individuation, autonomy, or inde-
pendence. First of all, it has less to do with a person's behavior
than, as mentioned, with his or her emotional being. Second,
there is a sense of connectedness to the concept that prevents
the mere gaining of distance or leaving, no less cutting off, from
being the way to achieve it. Third, as stated above, it has to do
with the fabric of one's existence, one's integrity.

A pastor's leadership, then, must become a natural, organic
function of the direction in which his life is already heading, of
his own "differentiation", if you will.   Otherwise, he will
always be susceptible to the disastrous scenarios already
described. We pastors risk forfeiting our leadership any time
we placate intimidating and intransigent people who covertly
undermine us as we naively stand by, or we fail to deal with
them swiftly because we fear a backlash or because we are pri-

vately unsure of ourselves and of our position. On the other hand, we cannot afford to become intimidating and intransigent ourselves by pushing or pulling others along instead of leading them with a clear, strong voice.

The dilemmas we face when attempting to navigate the shoals of evaluating and shaping our roles as power-brokers are several-fold. We desire to lead decisively and confidently, exercising personal initiative and a strong sense of stewardship concerning our responsibilities. Concurrently, we wish to relinquish control to God, to exhibit submission, humility and magnanimity toward our following. We may mistake weakness and passivity in ourselves for submission to God and others. After all, submission is a passive stance to some degree. Similarly, we may mistake our own bullheadedness for commitment. The answer is not in attempting to strike a balance between these poles as much as it is to see a third alternative altogether – leadership through self-differentiation.

Scratching my head one afternoon over these problems, I constructed a quadrant diagram. The horizontal axis is a continuum (from 0-10) representing congregational growth into commitment and initiative. The vertical axis is a continuum (from 0-10) representing congregational growth into submission and humility. The figures in each quadrant reflect whether or not the factor of submission and commitment are proportional to one another and, most importantly, how the functioning of the pastor (represented by the head) affects the 'body' or his followers. The diagram is meant to emphasize continuity and process rather than discrete categories. (The quadrants are not presented in numerical order.)

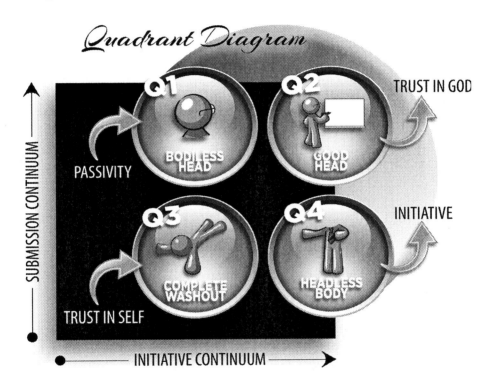

QUADRANT 1: The Bodiless Head

This quadrant is characterized by a strong, perhaps angry, self-styled leader who is demeaning and overly aggressive. The congregational body of such a head may prosper in times of duress or when the people are particularly in need of safety and security, and to remain intact they need a cause or something or someone to oppose. A potential danger here is the development of a Cult, which breeds on the militaristic, oppositional characteristics of a personality-based leader. The "bodiless head" creates, by definition, a climate where the pastor must over-function to survive, while his parishioners, often docile and detached from genuine participation, are only too happy to abdicate all responsibility to him. He is happy to take it all – until he burns out. An over-functioning pastor tends to create clones rather than disciples.

This congregation exists on the high end of the submission continuum, but there is minimum corresponding action or initiative on its part and therefore not a genuine submission being expressed. A passive church does not create a dominant pastor, however. On the contrary, the exact opposite is true. A dominant pastor always creates a passive people!

QUADRANT 4: The Headless Body

In this scenario the distinctiveness of the pastor – his leadership style, his philosophy of ministry, his vision – may create uneasiness and suspicion in members who themselves wield power in the congregation. A body of this type may be manipulated by a person or group of persons who are well entrenched and have a strong sense of ownership over the church's agenda. Any hesitancy on the part of the pastor will inevitably cause strong lay personalities to become inflamed in their opposition to focused leadership. This kind of body, where commitment to the emotional safety of the group is valued more than change and growth, is especially susceptible to the Jezebel problem and will, in general, tend to be less innovative and less likely to take risks. Because peace and togetherness are primary values in this body, an obstinate follower is often allowed too much leverage. (If "peace" is the primary value of your family, for instance, you may

We cannot afford to become intimidating and intransigent by pushing or pulling others along instead of leading them with a clear, strong voice.

fore-go previously made plans for the evening in deference to your screaming three-year-old.) Peace at the high price of progress may be the cost of group "headless body" leadership.

This congregation sits in the high end of the initiative continuum but low on the submission axis. Again, it is important to note that the weakness of the leader creates the necessary conditions for weakness in the congregation and not vice-versa. Weak fathers breed spoiled children, and not the other way around. A pastor may inherit a Quadrant IV or a Quadrant I church, but his consistent, well-differentiated leadership will ultimately result in a healthier, more functional people.

Paul glories in the fact that neither he nor his ministry has been diluted by undue peer influence.

QUADRANT 3: A Complete Washout

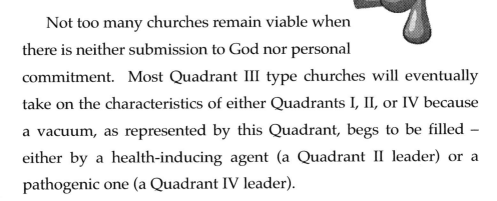

Not too many churches remain viable when there is neither submission to God nor personal commitment. Most Quadrant III type churches will eventually take on the characteristics of either Quadrants I, II, or IV because a vacuum, as represented by this Quadrant, begs to be filled – either by a health-inducing agent (a Quadrant II leader) or a pathogenic one (a Quadrant IV leader).

QUADRANT 2: The Body with a Good Head on its Shoulders

This body enjoys a leader who is well-positioned, one who is at once deeply connected to his people through mutual submission and yet differentiated from them by his own personal commitment. Our endeavor to be well-positioned calls for us to be engaged in two painful and soul-searching processes:

1. The quest to discover how our church is related to our own uniqueness as individuals, and

2. The imperative of dealing with sabotage to the above process.

The idea that our ministry is to some degree an extension of our individuality may seem at first to be narcissistic. Upon closer examination, however, we can clearly see that it is not. The Apostle Paul, uniquely prepared by personality, history, education, and revelation to be the torch-bearer to the Gentiles, could ill-afford to compare himself to the other apostles. His call was intensely personal and custom fit.

> But I make known to you, brethren, that the gospel which was preached by me is not according to man. For I neither received it from man, nor was I taught it, but it came through the revelation of Jesus Christ. For you have heard of my former conduct in Judaism, how I persecuted the church of

Peace at the high price of progress may be the cost of group "headless body" leadership.

God beyond measure and tried to destroy it. And I advanced in Judaism beyond many of my contemporaries in my own nation, being more exceedingly zealous for the traditions of my fathers. But when it pleased God, who separated me from my mother's womb and called me through His grace, to reveal His Son in me, that I might preach Him among the Gentiles, I did not immediately confer with flesh and blood, nor did I go up to Jerusalem to those who were apostles before me; but I went to Arabia, and returned again to Damascus.

Then after three years I went up to Jerusalem to see Peter, and remained with him fifteen days. But I saw none of the other apostles except James, the Lord's brother. –Galatians 1:11-19

For Paul to focus on what seemed to work elsewhere would have spelled his certain failure. In his letter he posits a number of considerations that, in his eyes, give credibility to him and to his ministry. First, his ministry is a result of a personal encounter with Christ, a product not of second-hand knowledge but of first-hand experience. Second, the Apostles ministry is grounded on the idea that it is unique in that both he and it have been set apart. Third, Paul glories in the fact that neither he nor his ministry has been diluted by undue peer influence.

At some point and in some way in our ministerial lives, each of us must push away from this pack – the consultants, the idea-generators, the church growth gurus, the successful models – and find out for ourselves who we are. To what specifically have I been called? How am I unique? What inherent qual[1]ities of leadership do I possess? As it was with both Paul and Jesus, perhaps the specter of personal failure or some other kind of wilderness experience is the Petri dish for this kind of self-discovery. To become an originator instead of merely an imitator takes great courage, long-term durability, and emotional maturity. By originator, I do not necessarily mean one whose structures, approaches or ideas are particularly novel or radically different, but one out of whose call, gifting, and vision these things appear, or are conceived, as natural by-products.

GETTING PERSONAL

- What am I called to create?

- Is this ministry I'm developing one that I would readily participate in if I were a layman?

- Is this ministry I'm developing one that I would readily participate in if I were an outsider?

- On our present course, will I love this church in ten years?

- Am I on an endless quest for new methods?

- Is this search an indication of my own lack of direction and conviction?

When a pastor can take a clear, specific stand based on the process of working out her own salvation, so to speak, she has no need to "motivate" others. She has no need to cajole, incite, placate, or appease. She simply goes to where she is going. The steady posture and pace of a confident leader creates her own attraction, her own following. I believe sure-footedness, while making us less vulnerable to overbearing people interested only in their own agenda, is also more apt to engender followers who discover their own niche in the scheme of things. Both pathogens of passivity and stubborn self-will are given less fuel to feed on when the leader is cohesive in her thinking and consistent in her actions.

At some point and in some way in our ministerial lives, each of us must push away from the pack—the consultants, the idea-generators, the church growth gurus, the successful models—and find out for ourselves who we are.

Opposition is inevitable, though. Resistance may [12]come not only because there is disagreement about our ideas or vision but because we dare to lead at all, especially if we have been too non-committal or have sounded an uncertain trumpet in the past. Those in the congregation who are most pastor-dependent will experience the most anxiety about their leader's "pull-out". For example, followers may instinctively respond to the loss of control they experience due to a reassertion of direction by their leader. When a pastor seeks to move her 'body' from Quadrant IV to Quadrant II, her followers may feel like she is moving to Quadrant I. She may be very tempted to maintain the status quo as the prospect of conflict becomes more imminent.

For some followers, the predictability of their leader is a source of great emotional comfort, and her personal renewal may therefore threaten them deeply, probably on a level they cannot articulate. Almost certainly the emotional tension will manifest itself in some "issue." It behooves the pastor at such times to be wise enough to see through the "issue" to the real problem: the knee-jerk emotional reaction of overly dependent followers. A leader must take a stand of quiet confidence and resist getting drawn into a war of wills. It is very difficult for any leader to create a challenging situation when she knows full well that to do so will stir up misunderstanding and adversity. This, however, is a test of leadership. Am I willing to allow the more dependent members of my church to experience pain? Can I handle their rejection if it comes to that? Just as we, the leaders, must be willing to walk through the wilderness of submission, loss and eventual rediscovery of self, so must our followers.

If we cannot bear to see our followers experience the pain of wilderness, we will cease to really lead them. If we fail to allow and sometimes even to precipitate pain in our followers, we become mere hirelings, therapeutic hand-holders, and false shepherds.

It is easy for a pastor to protect her members from pain and subsequent growth by failing to direct them specifically or to make her position unwaveringly clear. As she senses disgruntlement and resentment of followers whom she challenges, it is vital for her to maintain her position without being defensive, combative, or emotionally coercive. The quality of one's character when in the throes of conflict will ultimately determine her strength to lead when the dust settles.

Personal growth as a leader seems to come at the high price of having to determine what is ultimately important at crucial crossroads. Will we endure short-term upheaval for the sake of long-term fruitfulness? Can we stand up under the pain of confronting unpleasant realities, knowing very well we will disrupt the peace and our false sense of security? *The real challenge is not so much the prospect of confronting overbearing individuals as the trepidation of facing our fears and insecurities.*

Becoming a well-positioned leader is about searching out for ourselves what we believe about church life and acting decisively on our convictions. *When we seek to dominate because we are not really sure of ourselves or equivocate because we are not really sure of ourselves, we keep our churches in a state of perpetual infancy.* The only way to grow up is to lead us and our people through an acute and painful process of change.

As we all know, one of the factors that contributes to the gawkiness and lack of coordination in adolescents is that they are passing through puberty. Growing up as a leader is also a process of gaining strength in our muscles, giving our brains and emotions time to catch up 181with our lengthening limbs and to become familiar with and attuned to our own bodies. *Perhaps, when the cracks and squeaks have all been worked out of our developing vocal chords, we will one day discover that we have clearly and confidently come to recognize the sound of our own voice.* ❧

personal response

1. On a scale from 1-10 (1 being least likely, 10 being most likely), rate yourself in the area of defensiveness.

2. How defensive are you when someone questions or challenges you? In the depths of honesty, explain why.

3. Which quadrant does the church you currently attend (or pastor) fall under? 1, 2, 3 or 4? Explain.

4. In this ministry I'm developing, would I readily partici- pate in it if I were an outsider?

....

....

....

....

....

....

....

....

....

....

....

~~~~~~

assured

Truth divorced from experience
will always dwell in the realm of doubt.

–Henry Drause

~~~~~~

Chapter 6

Discerning Your Distinctive Calling

Foundations of Ministry

Therefore, brethren, be even more diligent to make your call and election sure, for if you do these things you will never stumble; for so an entrance will be supplied to you abundantly into the everlasting kingdom of our Lord and Savior Jesus Christ. —1 Peter 1:10-11

What makes you think you have a God-given call on your life?

This is the question that Paul is responding to in the book of Galatians. "Judaizers" have infiltrated the congregation at Galatia and have raised questions regarding Paul's credibility and calling. What were the cornerstones that provided the foundations for Paul's ministry? What, in Paul's mind, gives legitimacy to his apostleship? The following is Paul's response:

> But I make known to you, brethren, that the gospel which was preached by me is not according to man. For I neither received it from man, nor was I taught it, but it came through the revelation of Jesus Christ.
>
> For you have heard of my former conduct in Judaism, how I persecuted the church of God beyond measure and tried to destroy it. And I advanced in Judaism beyond many of my contemporaries in my own nation, being more exceedingly zealous for the traditions of my fathers. But when it pleased God, who separated me from my mother's womb and called me through His grace, to reveal His Son in me, that I might preach Him among the Gentiles, I did not immediately confer with flesh and blood, nor did I go up to Jerusalem to those who were apostles before me; but I went to Arabia, and returned again to Damascus. —Galatians 1:11-19

Paul puts his heart on the line and offers his best defense for why God is using him and why he should be taken seriously. I find six reference points for substantiating one's calling.

PERSONAL CALLING FLOWS FROM AN ENCOUNTER WITH CHRIST: *"It came through revelation..."*

We believe in Jesus. Our approach to ministry is always grounded in the fact that we serve a living God who relates to us personally. Only an experience with Christ is an adequate platform for viable ministry. We, like Paul, must know that our calling is from revelation, from encounter, and from first-hand experience.

Christianity is not merely a philosophy or ethic. It is not merely the commemoration of events or the preservation of rituals or scriptures. It is revelation and transformation.

What is the nature of your relationship with Christ? Have you encountered God?

PERSONAL CALLING FLOWS FROM DISCERNING ONE'S PAST: *"My Former Conduct..."*

Nothing is wasted with God. Our calling is anchored in all our experiences. There is no compartmentalization with God. Our future flows inextricably from our past. Our past is redeemed and we are new creatures, but it remains that our redeemed past plays a role in our calling. Paul knows this: his former conduct, his zeal, his passion for the scriptures, his Roman citizenship, his knowledge of the Greek culture and language, and his life as a Pharisee. All these factors provide the raw material for God's plan for his life.

Our ministry is crafted from our rib. Like Eve, our calling is not created out of nothing, but is the product of what already is. Dynamic life-ministry is a result of deep insight into what God has DONE and what He has DESIGNED in us. What He has done and designed leads us to what we will DO.

Have you considered your past through the eyes of retrospective faith? Do you see how God has uniquely prepared you for current assignments? Do you appreciate that God does not waste anything in your life?

Christianity
is not merely
a philosophy
or ethic.
It is not
merely the
commemoration
of events or
the preservation
of rituals or
scriptures.
Christianity is
revelation and
transformation.

PERSONAL CALLING FLOWS FROM

IDENTIFYING ONE'S PASSION: *"Being more exceedingly zealous..."*

We all have hot spots. Paul understood that deep reservoirs of passion fueled his activity before he knew Christ. These "fountains of the deep" make us who we are, even if they are misdirected and misunderstood without God. The Apostle's zeal was a point of continuity in his life. He had always had it. He understood his current assignment in the light of it. There are certain injustices that hit our emotional buttons.

There are certain unmet needs in our churches and in our communities that strike us in the heart.

We are all required to obey God whether we feel like it or not. However, there are God-designed concerns that resonate within us. When we tap these, our ministry is less wearing, less taxing and less burdensome because there are underground resources that we may draw from.

Do you understand and have you identified your passions in ministry? What must you do?

PERSONAL CALLING FLOWS FROM A RESPECT FOR GOD'S SOVEREIGNTY: *"Separated from my mother's womb..."*

Paul understood himself and his own makeup. He had a high level of self-awareness. At the same time he appreciated the fact that God was sovereign in his life. Calling flows from an intuitive "knowing" that God is working. Ministry is not merely "volunteerism" or one of many possible vocational choices based on one's personality or gifting. Personal calling is akin to water returning to the ocean: there is an inevitable sense of destiny and providence involved.

Deep respect for God's work and His preparation in one's life results in a sense of returning home. To be "called" is to experience a kind of homecoming experience: it's not about doing what I want to do as much as it is about becoming what I was created to be.

Do you recognize God's hand in your life? Do you experience awe and wonder at God's plans for you? If so, what practical measures should you take to insure that your life will reflect His handiwork?

PERSONAL CALLING FLOWS FROM SELF-DIFFERENTIATION: *"That I might preach Him among the Gentiles..."*

Paul was not a generalist. He knew precisely what he had been called to do. He was not apologetic, ambivalent, or tentative about it in any way.

He knew his target. He knew that Peter had been called to shepherd the Jews and lead them to a new understanding of their Messiah. He knew that he was called to the Gentiles by preparation and providence.

Knowing what you should not do and what you are unprepared for is the flip side of self-knowledge. It saves time and energy. Paul's focus was determined by what he was willing to fore-go, what he was willing to leave to others.

What makes you different? Are you willing to see your differences as a God-ordained advantage? Will you cave in to the pressures of conformity or will you allow your unique call and target to emerge?

Paul's focus was determined by what he was willing to fore-go; what he was willing to leave to others.

PERSONAL CALLING FLOWS FROM FIRST HAND EXPERIENCE: *"I did not confer with flesh and blood..."*

Anyone who does not learn from others is a fool. Proverbs 12:15 tells us, "The way of a fool is right in his own eyes, but he who heeds counsel is wise."

Paul had been a disciple of one kind or another all his life. He knew what it was to submit to the scrutiny of others.

Paul was most certainly a voracious learner, but he was no sycophant. He would not water down or dilute his own calling through mindless imitation or blind following. He insisted on having his own experiences with God.

We live in a world of mediated experiences. In our modern media culture, it is possible to live a second-hand life. We cannot afford, however, to have a plagiarized ministry. Genuine calling is person-specific, just like the incarnation is person-specific. We have nothing authentic to give unless we ourselves have lived it and gotten ourselves dirty with it.

The Word becomes flesh when we allow it to become processed through our lives. The essence of the word "witness" is the idea of first-hand familiarity. Personal calling is grounded in what we know because we are learning by living a great life, a life characterized by courage, curiosity and the pursuit of God. How many of us would choose to go to the Arabian

Desert rather than attend a conference where Peter and James were the keynote speakers?

Is your ministry balanced and seasoned with life experiences? Are you tempted to fake it? Are you tempted to minister beyond what you have really internalized and lived? How do you insure that you are not over-reaching and thus jeopardizing your credibility? ⌇

personal response

1. What makes you think you have a God-given call on your life? Our future flows inextricably from our past. In what areas do you sense that your redeemed past is playing a role in your calling?

2. Make a list of your "foundations of the deep" – your passions in ministry and why you think they won't leave you alone.

3. What makes you different and how might this help you identify your target in ministry? Expound.

4. Where has the "...Word become flesh" in your life? List experiences.

When you <u>actualize</u>
'who you are'
with purposeful behavior,
you will feel energized
and empowered.
–Sam Rockwell

He is most fatigued who knows
not what to do.
–Boileau

PART 2

Doing
Actualizes Being

~~~~~~~~~~~~~~~~~~~~~~~~~~~~~~~~~~~~~~~

priorities

If you could
once make up your mind
in the fear of God,
never to undertake more work
of any sort than you can carry on calmly,
quietly, without hurry or flurry,
and the instant you feel yourself
growing nervous, like one out of breath
would stop and take breath,
you would find this
simple common sense rule
doing for you what no prayers
or tears could ever accomplish.
—Elizabeth Prentiss

~~~~~~~~~~~~~~~~~~~~~~~~~~~~~~~~~~~~~~~

Spiritual Investment
Setting Ministry Priorities

And the things that you have heard from me

among many witnesses, commit these to faithful people

who will be able to teach others also. —II Timothy 2:2

This one verse crystallizes Paul's life and ministry. This simple directive, perhaps more clearly and succinctly than anything else Paul ever wrote, gives us the pivotal insight into what really counts in ministry.

The greatest apostle had a philosophy of investment. He did not scatter his seed. He planted it intentionally and purposefully. He spent most of his time, not with crowds, but with a few committed followers. Jesus and Paul impacted history, created world-changing leaders, and reached multiplied thousands by keeping to a few basic principles.

PAUL INVESTED IN FEW

The apostle's circle was relatively small: Silas, Apollo, Barnabus, Aquila, Priscilla, Luke, Timothy, Titus, and a few others. He poured himself out to many (Philippians 2:17, II Timothy 4:6) but invested only in a few (Philippians 2: 19-30). His most moving writings were addressed to his protégé's in the Pastoral Epistles. His greetings to Timothy, "My beloved, son" reflect the intensity and depth of relationship with his select few.

Paul's time was allocated to those who readily responded to him, to individuals who were moving toward him, to folks who were drawn into his orbit, so to speak. His energy was redeemed, not only through the disciplined use of time itself (Ephesians 5:16), but by the careful selection of who he was spending it with.

We invest in a few and expect them to reinvest in others. The question is: *Am I deliberate, prayerful, and prioritized in my selection and development of leaders?*

PAUL INVESTED IN THE CONTEXT OF COMMUNITY

The model that Paul and Jesus worked from was not an academic one where students sat, listened, and took notes. They worked from a master-disciple model where the learning was done in the context of community.

Paul reminds Timothy that there were many witnesses to his education. He is accountable not only to Paul, but also to others who have invested in his life. One of Paul's favorite themes is the idea of mutual learning and succession of faith (II Timothy 1:1-5).

Paul invested in people who were watched and measured by other leaders and investors (II Corinthians 3:2-3).

Am I deliberate, prayerful, and prioritized in my selection and development of leaders?

We learn together. The question is: *Am I a habitual learner, becoming accustomed to functioning on a team simultaneously as a peer and a student?*

PAUL INVESTED IN *REPRODUCERS*

"Do what I've done."

Paul does not mince words when it comes to what he expects from Timothy. He anticipates that his investment will produce results. He foresees the same process of succession and transference multiplying into the future.

The quality and nature of the disciple-making process is essentially and profoundly affected by the expectations of the leader. Is spiritual investment an exercise in delineating information or a process of reproduction? The answer to this question will qualify how we do everything.

Other translations of this verse use the term qualified and capable. The Apostle is essentially saying, *"You are responsible to invest in people who are competent to reproduce ministry."*

We expect fruitfulness and growth. *The question is: Am I investing in the process of individual and congregational multiplication?*

PAUL INVESTED AS A *MENTOR*

The word "teach" creates different images in our minds than it did in first century learners. Teaching was a life-based experience. Paul lectured and spoke publicly, but his instruction to Timothy was of the "just in time" variety. The Pastoral Epistles are great examples of this. All of Paul's teaching was a response to the particular challenges of the moment.

A mentor comes alongside and offers personal perspective and wisdom. Timothy was no mere student; he was the recipient of Paul's heart and affection (II Timothy 1:2; 4:9-12).

Our approach is relational. The question is: *Am I investing in other leaders/pastors in life-related ways? Am I developing people or am I merely delegating tasks?*

PAUL INVESTED WITH A *MULTI-GENERATIONAL PERSPECTIVE*

In Timothy, Paul saw the future. He was seeing four spiritual generations ahead: From me to you and *to faithful men who will teach others also.* A shortsighted ministry aims for the BIG BANG but not for the L O N G H A U L . Much of the discouragement we experience in ministry today is due to event-related myopia. Paul's contribution was oriented toward relational process, ministry succession, and generational continuity. How could one bad service or one bad sermon endanger that?

We make decisions based on the long-term view. The question is: *What is ultimately best for the church and its enduring ministry?*

These reference points elicit the following questions that should determine your ministry priorities. They are:

1. **We invest in a few and expect them to reinvest in others.** The question is: Am I deliberate, prayerful, and prioritized in my selection and development of leaders?

2. **We learn together.** The question is: Am I a habitual learner, becoming accustomed to functioning on a team simultaneously as peer and student?

3. **We expect fruitfulness and growth.** The question is: Am I investing in the process of individual and congregational multiplication? ࿔

personal response

1. Paul made it a holy habit to always be deliberate, prayerful and prioritized in choosing what? Explain his motive as you see it.

2. In the leadership model we are studying in this chapter, leaders should not only be a peer, but also a student. Why would it be difficult for some leaders to hesitate at simultaneously being a student? Expound.

3. A shortsighted ministry aims for the BIG BANG but not for the L O N G H A U L . What one primary principle will help them expand their vision? Explain.

....

....

....

....

....

....

....

....

....

counsel

The quality of the people closest to you
is the most accurate indicator
of the quality of your future.
–Sam Rockwell

Chapter 8

Recognizing Primary Relationships

Creating a Powerful Circle

After these things the Lord appointed seventy others also, and sent

them two by two before His face into every city and place where He

Himself was about to go…Then the seventy returned with joy, say-

ing, "Lord, even the demons are subject to us in Your name."

—*Luke 10:1, 17*

*M*any people use the word 'ministry' pretty loosely and without any clear understanding of what it really is. I think of the guy who walked into the pastor's office and says, "I've failed at all my attempts to start my own business, I'm currently unemployed. I am considering the ministry."

Some people see ministry as the last ditch effort for successful work if all else fails. Others see it is a highly exalted enterprise full of praise and glory. Neither of these extremes is a realistic perspective.

WHAT IS MINISTRY ANYWAY?

Let me offer a working definition for use here. **Ministry:** *a service or activity that enhances life; practical help that meets a perceived need; physical, spiritual or emotional support; "other-focused" activity; equipping and encouraging people to pursue God-centered dreams and plans; to facilitate God's will in the lives of others.*

Ministry is not just a voca-

Jesus did ministry
as a way of life
but first He did
ministry
as a way of being.
It was, and is still,
an essential
element of
who He is.
Out of His being
came His doing.

---

tional calling for a few. Ministry is how we are each called to live as disciples of Christ. On some level most of us know this, but the word and the associations we have connected to it can sometimes be intimidating and confusing. Another description of ministry is simply this: ministry is bringing help from God into the lives of people on earth. Help in time of need. Ultimately, ministry is bringing the Kingdom of God into our immediate experience. Ministry comes out of how we live first with God and is then a natural reflection then of how we live with others. It is therefore more than a sacred profession, though it is that also.

> *You are a chosen people. You are royal priests, a holy nation, God's very own possession. As a result, you can show others the goodness of God, for He called you out of the darkness into His wonderful light.*
> —*1 Peter 2:9, New Living Translation*

Ministry in this context is made to be done in a community of believers and is meant to be a "team effort". We are made to be a "chosen people, royal priests, a holy nation" not simply a collection of holy individuals, but a body of individuals knit together and working together to bring the Kingdom of God to the lost and hurting world we live in. With that in mind, ministry as I'm talking about it here is the more formal, trained approach - part of an organized body of people who worship and serve together in a regular and public way. As much as Jesus did ministry stemming out of His individual self, He also practiced it in intentional, cultivated community.

HOW DID JESUS DO MINISTRY?

Jesus did ministry as a way of life but first He did ministry as a way of being. It was, and is still, an essential element of who He is. Out of His being came His doing. As an extension of the ministry that came out of Himself, He then multiplied ministry through a network, a team, and a circle. He was the master of discerning primary relationships and strategically developing them. Jesus was invested in reproducing Himself through others. This may seem obvious but it's important recognise that Jesus deeply valued individuals (consider the parable of the Shepherd going to look for one lost sheep) and yet also valued groups of individuals that were interconnected with Him and interconnected with each other.

Jesus viewed ministry as a God-directed ("I do nothing of Myself; but as My Father taught Me..." John 8) and people-centered ("Jesus had compassion" Luke 20) enterprise.

The dynamics of these interrelated social connections form the invisible, yet most important, components of creating ministry. Learning how to discern and develop our own primary relationships is central to everything else we do in disciple making.

A NETWORK

How do you define a 'network'? Is it some multilevel, pyramid scheme kind of thing? Is it something you strategically build or is something more organic than that? Well, yes and no to all of the above. A good working definition of a network is "all the people you know and mobilize toward a common cause". It is multi-level but it is also unilateral and interconnected to dozens of people you already know and have real relationships with. Yes, you do strategically build it as you develop key relationships and encourage the development of relationships between others in the same system. But it is also organic and naturally developing as people are naturally attracted to others of their own kind, their own interests and values. In a sense, a network is really like a super large family, even a tribe. The dynamic nature of a network multiplies the resources of all within the network and all those resources - the capital, the know-how, the gifts, and the energy we need to do God's will, lies within the power of the network. This is one of the reasons that our functioning successfully in the Body is so important to God and why He puts us in community to begin with!

Networks are not a new idea, contrary to what you might think. The idea didn't come from marketing majors or sales gurus. God started the use of networks (interlinked groups of people serving a common cause) early in our history and has always worked through family systems, clans, and tribes. So don't be intimidated by the idea of tapping into a network or managing one! It is core to the growth of all ministry and to healthy corporate life in Christ.

> *"Your fathers went down to Egypt with seventy persons, and now the LORD your God has made you as the stars of heaven in multitude."* —*Deuteronomy 10: 22*

> *Then Moses went up, also Aaron, Nadab, and Abihu, and seventy of the elders of Israel, and they saw the God of Israel."* —*Exodus 24: 9-10*

> *After these things the Lord appointed seventy others also, and sent them two by two before His face into every city and place where He Himself was about to go...Then the seventy returned with joy, saying, "Lord, even the demons are subject to us in Your name."* —*Luke 10:1, 17*

A network can only be utilized to its fullest for a cause that benefits everyone. The rallying cry that brings a network together and galvanizes them into a real unit must go out for a purpose higher and greater than any one member of the network. Vision and selflessness are the characteristics of anyone who seeks to mobilize and unleash the latent potential of one's network. To vision cast and lead a network your core desire must be to fulfill the vision while bringing every member of the network into greater fulfillment of their own capacities and potential.

Name 15-25 people in your life that you will share your mission with. These are people with whom you share core values and interests, the same kind of hopes for a greater purpose, the same vision for the outworking of God in our world. These will be people that you feel a "kinship" with even if you haven't spent a lot of concerted time together. Naming each of them in a tangible way – writing their names down – gives you a new kind of ownership and hand of authority in creating a viable network. Think about who they are as individuals and what God

The common thread that binds a team is a fiercely held goal that each member takes ownership of and is willing to lay down their own agenda for.

may be calling them to. Pray over them and listen to what God tells you His plans and purposes are for them.

For vision to be anything more than a dream, it must be shared and received. Your network, those people who you already know, is the place to begin.

A TEAM

A team is a smaller, more strategically fitted set of people with a more clearly defined purpose to which all are joined and can only be achieved with the full cooperation of each other. Teams are made up of hand-picked individuals with widely varying gifts and skills often with little redundancy. The common thread that binds a team is a fiercely held goal that each member takes ownership of and is willing to lay down their own agenda for. Character and virtue become the qualities that are similarly shared even while sporting very different abilities and temperaments.

> *Now it came to pass in those days that He went out to the mountain to pray, and continued all night in prayer to God. And when it was day, He called His disciples to Himself; and from them He chose twelve whom He also named apostles.*
> *–Luke 6:12-13*

Jesus employed a reproducible model of team recruitment and deployment. This is a model we can study and we can duplicate.

He prayed at length for the team

Just like you need to be praying over the individuals that make up your network, you need to pray over the members of your team. Who are they – what is their special identity? What do they need while serving on the team and what do they need when they are not actively engaged in the team's efforts? What are their individual weaknesses, their strengths, their points of vulnerability? What does God envision that they each can become? How can you serve and lead them to that?

He called his disciples "from" something "to" something

He closed the deal. To become a member of a team – a Special Forces unit, if you will – means to leave something behind in order to take up something new. Are you calling potential team members with the clear understanding that they are giving up something, and probably something of value to them, so that they can take up the something you are bringing them into? Do you have a clear idea of the value of what you are asking of them so that there is integrity in what is being given in exchange for their sacrifices? Make sure that you are leading people to something better than what they are leaving behind. That doesn't mean that you can guarantee success of the vision or the individual. It does mean that you have to be clear that God is the author of the vision and you are serving Him as you work for it.

He selected them carefully

Choosing team members is not based on snap decisions or quick choices. Really look and evaluate those whom you choose to serve with you and the rest of the team. Are the essential core qualities strong and self-sustaining in each of them? Are they humble, willing to serve, capable, trustworthy, good company? Will they work well with others? Will they be able to forgive other team members when they make mistakes or hurt them? Will they be generous or will they be demanding? All these issues matter and will impact the outcome of the team's efforts.

He immediately conceived them as "apostles"

He didn't choose "assistants," He chose leaders.

Empowering and releasing these key individuals was something that was pre-meditated by Jesus and is a pattern we must use ourselves if we are really going to grow sustainable and thriving teams. People will bring their very best gifts (and sometimes failings) to the table when they are actually responsible for real outcomes. They will rise to meet the level of expectation given for them. Jesus knew that and boldly employed that model with a set of guys that didn't look remotely like they could pull anything off. But they were carefully chosen because of what was hidden in their hearts and spirits, and because they were empowered from the beginning to be leaders, they became leaders exceeding all expectations!

Name the 4-8 people that are emerging as part of your team. What are their strengths? What are their roles? How do they speak into your vision? What do you see them doing that they can't yet see? How are you preparing them for the future? Do you get them together as a team? Do they know who the other members of the team are? Do you have a clear plan of what you are leading them to do? Are you prepared to be responsible for that leadership?

A CIRCLE

Now after six days Jesus took Peter, James, and John his brother, led them up on a high mountain by themselves; and He was transfigured before them. His face shone like the sun, and His clothes became as white as the light. —Matthew 17: 1-2

While He was still speaking, some came from the ruler of the synagogue's house who said, "Your daughter is dead. Why trouble the Teacher any further?" As soon as Jesus heard the word that was spoken, He said to the ruler of the synagogue, "Do not be afraid; only believe." And He permitted no one to follow Him except Peter, James, and John the brother of James.

These few Jesus chose carefully; He selectively shared Himself. Jesus made Himself vulnerable to these few not because they would not fail or hurt Him, but because they each had the capacity to rise again from failure.

Then He came to the house of the ruler of the synagogue, and saw a tumult and those who wept and wailed loudly. When He came in, He said to them, Why make this commotion and weep? The child is not dead, but sleeping."
–Mark 5:35-39

And He took Peter, James, and John with Him, and He began to be troubled and deeply distressed. Then He said to them, "My soul is exceedingly sorrowful, even to death. Stay here and watch." He went a little farther, and fell on the ground, and prayed that if it were possible, the hour might pass from Him. –Mark 14: 33-35

"You will indeed drink the cup that I drink, and with the baptism I am baptized with you will be baptized..." –Mark 10:39

Jesus trained a few to take His place.

He employed these principles:

He revealed himself and became vulnerable to the inner circle

These few He chose carefully and selectively shared Himself. He made Himself vulnerable to these few not because they would not fail or hurt Him, but because they each had the capacity to rise again from failure and to be changed into something more. He lived out His life in front of these men but He also was willing for them to see His future glory. He was willing lay down not His life for them, but His emotional safety. Can you choose 3 to 8 people with whom you are willing to do the same?

He provided lessons and experiences that were special to them

Jesus was purposeful about providing staged mentoring and careful guidance that would be unique to those few. He sought revelation from His Father on their behalf and modeled the fullness of being both Man and God with them. Will you commit to seeking the Lord on behalf of a chosen few to find what is most needed to teach them? Will you be willing to be filled with God on their behalf and let them see it?

He prayed for and with them

Prayer is preeminent. It must precede all other actions. It creates the groundwork on which everything else is built in these relationships and opens up avenues of relationship that can come no other way. Praying together binds relationships together in ways that no amount of talking to each other will ever do. It is the seal of the Spirit that awakens the spirit in each and calls to unity and revelation. Can you cultivate that with discipline and faithfulness with these few?

He endured and overcame their betrayal

Inevitably, our closest and most beloved will at some time fail and betray us. It is the nature of our race until the Lord finishes His great redemptive work. Can you love those who fail you, even betray you, and hold to your commitment of love in that small circle? Can you model long-suffering love like Jesus did with His small circle of frail men who would later grow to become giants among men and lead His sheep? Can you allow for failure amongst this small group and still leave the door open to continued intimacy with them?

He asked and expected more from them

Jesus was explicit about His expectations with His disciples and even though they did not always understand what He was asking of them, He asked nevertheless. The asking and the expecting create the standard and boundaries of what our relationships become. Can you ask openly for what you expect of your inner circle, forgive when it isn't met but continue to expect and not deviate from the core standard that must be met? This is how we give those we love the map to become the best of themselves in relationship to us. It is true for inner circles, close friendships, marriage, children, and strong business relationships. Be clear about what you expect and need. It takes faith and courage to ask like this. Be bold!

Who are you reproducing your ministry in? Who are the 3-8 people that you are investing you life in? List them. Do they know it? Do you know why have you chosen them? Do you know what you investing and what you are hoping to see produced?

In closing let me offer some observations from my experience with developing networks, teams and circles of relationships.

OBSERVATIONS

- One wrong person in your life or your team can wreak havoc. Consider what to place the greatest value on in members of your team. Someone who is high maintenance – not necessarily overtly contentious or strife creating, but demanding, needy or fundamentally unskilled for their role on the team will probably not be a good fit regardless of their gifting or eagerness to be a part of it. No amount of prayer and counsel can make someone fit who doesn't have the essential qualities needed before they come on the team. Skills can be taught but solid character and complementing temperament have to pre-exist. Humility, service, and good judgment may not seem like very exciting qualities but they are priceless in team dynamics.

- **Don't tolerate strife.** (Strife is created when people don't respect others, their position or their leadership.) Be swift to deal with this. Make sure your team knows what the chain of command is and how to function within it. Be proactive in expressing your policy about how grievances are managed up the chain of command, not sideways or down the chain of command. Build unity and accord among the team.

- **Beware of seduction and sabotage.** These forces come into play much more subtly than obvious strife or disrespect. Keep yourself clear of any guilt first. Be diligent about confessing your own sin, and being cleansed of it. Seduction can't find a foothold if you don't give it one. Listen to your gut when you start to feel those red-flags going up inside about sabotage. Your gut is rarely wrong. Don't dismiss that warning out of hand thinking you're overreacting or reading too much into something. Keep your eyes open. Get discreet feedback and confirmation from others. But be careful how you handle that so you don't end up spreading suspicion. Remember that the real enemy is not your team members but the devil. The devil loves to use people against each other, to accuse, to fan the flames of envy and power hunger. Remembering where you stand with God is the best way to ward off the enemy's tactics.

- **Don't promote someone with a bad attitude or who is not respectful, no matter how gifted or charismatic they are.** Toxic talk, bitterness, or resentment can destroy a team from the inside out. Deal with it directly, firmly, and decisively. Left unattended it will erode the respect of individuals for your leadership. If someone is disrespectful or frequently contentious confront them about this. If it continues, lovingly and constructively help them "de-select".

- **When it comes to people – subtraction is as powerful as addition.** More is not always – well – more. Sometimes team synergy works best when there are fewer people and the trust is higher amongst a tighter framework of people. In instances where someone just doesn't fit, don't be afraid to make decisive choices about removing someone or redirecting them to other areas of service. If someone isn't really successfully contributing to the overall vision and unity of the team, the likelihood is high that they know it themselves and may not know how to excuse themselves or to find where they might fit better.

- **It is better to risk being betrayed by a few than to withhold trust from those who've earned it.** In other words, take a risk of getting hurt by extending trust as an act of faith, even when you know that the person you are trusting may falter. Failing in performance is something that can be covered with grace and come back from. Failing for lack of integrity is not.

When it comes to people - subtraction is as powerful as addition.

- **People are trusted who trust.** Like begets like. Demonstrate trust and honor in order to cultivate those qualities in others.

- **Play to each other's strengths and cover each other's weaknesses.** One of the great principles of building a thriving organization – whether it is a family, a church, a ministry network, or a business – is to not focus on correcting individual's weaknesses, but building on their strengths and covering as a team for the individual weaknesses. Playing to each other's strengths allows a tremendous synergy of winning to happen and the taste of winning, of operating in your power alley, feeds itself. When people are giving their best and being received that way, instead of having their weaknesses point out, a power emerges that can be downright startling. The happiest teams that work together most successfully and sustainably are the ones who can recognise each other's weaknesses but work off each other's strengths. It is without a doubt a more positive approach and it uses far less energy than trying to be compensating for what team members can't do because they are put into the wrong spot or asked to carry the wrong task. This is worth all the thought you put into understanding the strengths and weaknesses of your team members. ꒰

personal response

1. Some people see ministry as the last ditch effort for successful work if all else fails. Others see it is a highly exalted enterprise full of praise and glory. Neither of these extremes is a real picture of it. From your heart, describe your perception of ministry. Expound.

2. From page 148, *"Jesus did ministry as a way of life but first He did ministry as a way of being."* What does this statement mean to you? Expound.

3. Jesus was explicit about His expectations with His disciples and even though they did not always understand what He was asking of them, He asked nevertheless. The asking and the expecting create the standard and boundaries of what our relationships become. Can you ask openly - fearlessly - for what you expect of your inner circle? Expound.

4. Very gifted, anointed and/or charsmatic people are attractive. Their gifts are those accompanied also by the gift of influence. Is it a good idea to promote these gifted ones when their attitude is all whacked out? If your answer is "No," please explain.

~~~~~~

teamwork

Coming together is a beginning.
Keeping together is progress.
Working together is success.
–Henry Ford

~~~~~~

Chapter 9

Building
A Working Team
How Successful Teams are Formed

But now [are they] many members, yet but one body.

— 1 Corinthians 12:20-25

Team building is the process we employ to build people. It is the main thing. Teamwork isn't incidental to the task -- it is primary to the task. When we say we organize ourselves in teams it means we arrange accountability, responsibility, and support around a common purpose, a real set of values, and a leader. It means that relationships and values serve as the glue that holds and binds us together – not primarily the task, not primarily the leader.

The following is an attempt to communicate a different way of doing things. We want to change the way we accomplish work in the church. The work is important. How we accomplish the work is just as important.

Often, the church is an extension of the ministry of the pastor, or worse, the church serves as an audience for the ministry of the pastor. The pastor, however, is but one gift in the multi-gifted community of the church. The problem is not that the pastor is hoarding, or intentionally monopolizing the mission of the church. The problem is not usually ill-motivation on her part, but a frustrating dilemma that can be illustrated by this simple predicament.

A car mechanic loves to work on cars so much that he becomes the proprietor of his own shop. Disaster soon erupts because no one is doing the books, scheduling the work, handling the customers, or ordering new parts because the owner is always under the hood of a car. If the business is to survive, the mechanic must resist the urge to do what his training has taught him – repair cars – and learn to manage the shop. Likewise, a pastor must arrange the church to do the work of the ministry, not assemble a gallery of spectators for his own. It is the non-public, quiet work of creating a great team that will determine the most important factors impacting a congregation's future.

The process of releasing the church to do the ministry entails more than mere delegation or management. Delegation is about task assignments. Assigning tasks and supervising work is important, but it is only a small part of reproducing ministry in the church. The goal is to replicate life-giving relationships and networks of community that get ministry done in a way that is consistent with recognized values – values that are reinforced in the activity of the team.

Selecting, developing, and cultivating a team is the first job of anyone in ministry at any level.

So what does this mean? It means that selecting, developing, and cultivating a team is the first job of anyone in ministry at any level. The

ministry not only gets done, but it gets done in a healthy, rela-
tionship-oriented, reproducing way. It means that we don't
organize our church around programs, but around teams. We
have programs, but the organizing principle is teams reproducing teams, not the program itself. This involves a different way
of "seeing." We see the team first – it's relational structure, it's
life together, it's unique makeup and assignment– before we see
the program it develops or the ministry it serves. The ministry
gets done in all kinds of creative, programmatic and non-pro-
grammatic ways while maintaining (actually generating) a
dense, fully relational infrastructure.

WHAT ARE THE PRINCIPLES AND VALUES THAT UNDER-GIRD THIS PHILOSOPHY OF MINISTRY?

*Everyone should have a close, supportive circle of team-
mates.* The church should be a place where community, friendships and lifelong working relationships are developed. The
working group that one creates to do ministry should be select-
ed and employed based on the expectation that the team will
endure for as long as it remains viable.

The team works together indefinitely. The idea is not to
"divide" and start new groups but to develop the leadership
potential of each member and multiply teams accordingly.

The leader selects and develops the team. A leader begins with the understanding that he/she is gathering a group of potential team leaders. This ministry determines the initial impetus of the team. He/she presents the team with certain ministry goals and they form a plan of action. The varied responsibilities are divided and shared. A team member's gifts and interests indicate what kind of team will subsequently form as a result of the part one plays in the first team.

The capacity of a team to be focused is determined by the leader's capacity for self-clarification. A leader must be able to say, "This is what God has called me to do." The "how" of that assignment is fodder for the team. The leader should not command the details. He/she must, however, be precise as to what the overarching purpose of the team is. A team without a clear-headed leader will founder.

The commitment to being a team member is a determining factor for everyone. Discerning one's gifting and passion are very important and key ingredients, but building teams is the means by which our gifts and passions are perpetuated beyond our own energy, indeed beyond our own lifetime. We value the gift, but we value the willingness to reproduce that gift by working with others even more.

The goal is to participate on two teams. On the first team, a member serves as a peer to the others while serving the ministry of the leader. The second team gathers as a result of the clarity and assignment one receives on the first team. On the second team, one serves as a coach and leader to the rest of the members.

Adequate time and attention should be given to the first team. The prospect of launching a successful second team pivots on the strength, insight, and inspiration members receive from the first team. A new team leader's passions, gifts, and character are tested among his colleagues. He is then empowered and "sent out" to build a new team, while maintaining his supportive relationship with the original group and its leader. The frequency of the first team's meetings may decrease as the second team is being developed, or they may not.

The motivation for team building should ultimately be a deep compassion for a world in need of Christ.

Praying for workers to be added to the team is "job one" for everyone. Not everyone is a recruiter. Not everyone will excel at gathering people for the sake of a cause. Everyone, however, can pray in accordance with Matthew Chapter 9. Each person in ministry can be involved in building teams that build people by praying for "laborers to be sent into the harvest."

The motivation for team building should ultimately be a deep compassion for a world in need of Christ. In other words, we are motivated into ministry by love for people and obedience to God, not position, ego, our gifts and interests, or even our need to be useful. We are compelled by love and this is why we create supportive networks. To be oriented and motivated by "us" in contrast to "me" helps insure that the ministry performed is pure and lasting.

A strong team emerges when it is equally committed to "being" and "doing". A team should have a task, whether called to serve the church, or the greater community outside the church. An important aspect of the team's work is to polish its focus and get something done. At the same time, a team is vigilant to respond to the personal needs of each member. An exclusively task-oriented team will turn sterile and fail to inspire and replenish its members. On the other hand, a group that exists only to hang out becomes inbred and is easily distracted by overly needy individuals.

Building teams is a natural form of growth and reproduction. Relationships need not be contrived when we are free to build teams based on God's guidance and our own sense of affinity and friendship. The church grows because we are forming healthy community, not because we are building a house of cards that relies on bigger and better programming.

Building teams saves the leader from burnout due to over-functioning. The leader should take responsibility, help bring focus to the team, define her calling and purpose clearly, and plan for the future. The leader cannot do all the work, see all the needs, or provide all the answers. When the team leader attempts to function in a heroic fashion, he/she unintentionally undermines the values of love and community he/she is trying to promote.

Building teams helps the leader to focus on a few people and a few priorities. Our commitment is to invest in a few who will invest in a few, and so on. The needs and demands of the church are always great. The animating force behind our work should not be the perpetual urgency of a needy congregation, but an intentional and deliberate strategy of giving attention to a few potential leaders.

One's life message is most vividly expressed in the accomplishments of those served. This is the premise that multiplying ministry through teams finds as its foundation. The ministry of the church should be marked by genuine life-change and substantial investment in the lives of people. Your contribution is fully realized, not so much in what you do directly, but in whether those under your care flourish. ᘒ

personal response

1. From the information provided in this chapter, in a sentence or two, write down your own definition of "team."

2. In what ways have you monopolized areas of your ministry in the past where you should be arranging teams to do the work of the ministry? Be brutally honest.

3. Who are your close-knit circle of supportive teammates? Name them.

4. What things do you need to change and/or modify in order to model the building of a team of team builders?

5. How will your life change when strong teams are carrying out the work of the ministry?

....

....

....

....

answerability

Everyone needs a bottom line
of some sort; everyone needs to be
responsible, accountable to
whomever it is they are serving.

—Bob Buford

Chapter 10

Serving in a Supportive Role

Issues of Integrity

Let nothing be done through selfish ambition or conceit,
but in lowliness of mind let each esteem others better than himself.
Let each of you look out not only for his own interests,
but also for the interests of others. —*Philippians 2:3-4*

*S*upporting a leader in a staff position demands a level of commitment and allegiance that goes beyond merely being a good church member. Staff people are targets of occasional (and sometimes unrelenting) congregational disgruntlement. The associate leaders are the first to hear potentially divisive comments, ranging from questions about the leader's personal life to misgivings on how the pastor's spouse styles his/her hair.

Not only is the associate the first to face budding opposition to the leader, he/she gets a front row seat to the very real vulnerabilities and limitations of the one in charge. It is no exaggeration to say that the integrity of key team members is one of the most critical issues facing a church's health and viability.

The fundamental question then, is this: How does one initially establish and then maintain integrity as a support person? How do you make your "calling and election sure" in this most significant role?

There are four questions that must be grappled with when deciding whether or not to take on a staff position in a church. They need to be addressed, not only before one begins the new assignment, but all along the way:

1. *Do I want to go where this leader is going?*
   This question addresses the pastor's vision for the future. Do we share the same mental picture of what the future should hold? Do we share the same metaphors and images, or do I prefer different ones? Do I find myself wishing that another ministry or another leader will influence the pastor and that he will adjust the ministry plan accordingly?

2. *Do I believe what this leader believes?*
   Is there doctrinal agreement? Are the written values of

the church being expressed in the life of the leader? Agreement on values is the key to compatibility. The leader's vision and mission may evolve and develop over time, but values are hard-wired to a great extent. It is important to discern, not just the written or stated values but the functional ones as well. What is really important to this leader?

3. *Do I like him/her on a personal level?*

   This is more important than one might imagine. I may admire a leader's success, gifts or position, but if I recoil at his/her personality or style, I'm going to find myself being less than enthusiastic. A pastoral staff position demands, by definition, an eagerness to be personally supportive.

4. *Can I serve this leader wholeheartedly?*

   Support leaders serve as one of the most telling indicators to the congregation of how well or "not well" things are going. My role as associate, to a large degree, is to exemplify and personify what the pastor is trying to accomplish. If I am anything less than totally committed, my hesitancy will be amplified and exaggerated beyond what I may be able to recognize. My heart will be read like a book, whether I mean for it to be or not.

If you cannot answer these questions affirmatively, you

should not sign up for the job. Sometimes prospective support people will convince themselves that even if they do not entirely endorse a leader, they can remain loyal publicly. They believe they can function integrally within the prescribed role and resist undermining the leader, despite harboring private reservations. Sometimes the opportunity to pursue personal dreams, develop underutilized gifts, or simply have a job makes it difficult to fully address unpleasant contradictions. Failure to be ruthlessly honest may eventuate in personal and professional disaster down the road. Integrity demands thoughtful self-definition along with due diligence in assessing a pastor's heart to determine whether or not there is a "match."

Ultimately, one's colors will show. One can certainly function supportively while not intentionally or maliciously eroding trust in the leader, but uncertainty will manifest itself in the rough and tumble of day-to-day conflicts and challenges. It is inevitable that a staff person who is not unreservedly present will weaken the pastor and the church.

What if you find yourself in a compromised position? If your answer to any of the following questions is "yes", you may have to make some difficult decisions about your future.

- Do you feel the need to subtly distinguish yourself from the pastor in key areas?

- Do you feel unsettled in the church?

- Have you confided misgivings about the pastor or church to someone in the church?

- Do you feel resentful toward the pastor?

If you are going to experience God's blessing and trust in the future, it is imperative that during a time of testing and personal frustration you act circumspectly and ethically. It is a common experience to feel powerless and angry when serving a leader you do not believe in. These feelings must not be used as an excuse for acting in a way that damages the church or the pastor. Here are some suggestions if you are at an impasse:

It is inevitable that a staff person who is not unreservedly present will weaken the pastor and the church.

- Have an honest conversation with your leader.

- Determine whether your issues are significant based on the four questions listed above.

- If they are, take full responsibility for not discerning areas of incompatibility earlier in the relationship.

- Do not take these issues to anyone else in the church. You are a steward of all the friendships you enjoy within the church. These relationships are based on the trust you have been given to represent your leader to them. No matter how lonely or victimized you may feel, you are not justified in violating the trust of your pastor.

- Take the bullet. If you need to resign and leave your position, it is your responsibility to leave without doing damage. Your future and your integrity rest squarely on negotiating this difficult transition.

When leaders go separate ways it is almost always because of a change in direction or some type of conflict. If the pastor's moral or ethical behavior is at issue, then additional measures are required. Two or more people with first-hand knowledge should validate inappropriate conduct on the part of the pastor. An overseer, elder, and/or outside counsel should be contacted and an ethics committee may review the situation. Even in an extreme case when the pastor is ethically or morally at fault, an associate must be very careful to be discreet and respectful.

To be tested in a subordinate role is not an unusual experience. In fact, it is a common strategy for God to take as He prepares and develops a leader. God tested David with an almost impossibly difficult situation with King Saul. David was not allowed to "touch God's anointed." God's standards for someone in a support role are extremely high. Therefore, it is as important for the staff person to be directed by sound wisdom in choosing a leader as it is for the leader to be clearly directed in choosing staff. ◁

personal response

1. How do you know that you want to go where your pastor/leader is going?

2. Do you deeply believe what your pastor/leader believes? Why?

3. Do you like your pastor/leader on a personal level? Expound.

4. In what ways can you serve your pastor/leader wholeheartedly?

5. Are there issues in your heart, which may distract, delay, or dilute any of the four items listed above? If so, what are they and what do you intend to do about them?

becoming

What you do when you don't have to,
determines what you will be
when you can no longer help it.
-- Rudyard Kipling

Practicing for Longevity
Essential Habits for Life

The LORD said to Samuel, "Do not look at his appearance

or at the height of his stature, because I have refused him.

For the LORD does not see as man sees;

for man looks at the outward appearance,

but the LORD looks at the heart —1 Samuel 16:7

The kind of leadership we are trying to promote is not the kind we usually imagine: the epic, heroic kind of leadership that asserts itself and takes charge. We are talking about the kind that Jesus exemplified and encouraged, the kind that emerges from a life that follows Christ with passion and integrity.

Leadership is more about how to follow well than it is

about getting your way. It is more about servanthood than it is about assertiveness or authority or even competence.

Jesus called them to Himself and said,

> *"You know that the rulers of the Gentiles lord it over them, and those who are great exercise authority over them. Yet it shall not be so among you; but whoever desires to become great among you, let him be your servant. And whoever desires to be first among you, let him be your slave; just as the Son of Man did not come to be served, but to serve, and to give His life a ransom for many." —Matthew 20: 25-28*

Leadership that emerges as a result of a life well lived has lasting effects and always promotes and serves others. Leadership that is a product of "having to be first" instead of "serving from the heart" does more harm than good.

When the requirements of leadership are carefully examined, it loses its glamour and some of its appeal. It is not about getting your way. Spiritual leadership is all about giving your way away!

> *"My brethren, let not many of you become teachers, knowing that we shall receive a stricter judgment." —James 3: 1*

Jesus to Peter:

> *"Most assuredly, I say to you, when you were younger, you*

girded yourself and walked where you wished; but when you are old, you will stretch out your hands, and another will gird you and carry you where you do not wish." —*John 21: 18*

These "practices" are designed to make us better followers of Christ before they are designed to make us leaders. The best kind of leadership is a by-product of following the ultimate Leader, not a consequence of personal ambition, envy or strife.

The "practices" are listed as they occurred to me. I'm not attempting to be profound or comprehensive; these are simply things that

Spiritual leadership is not about getting your way. Spiritual leadership is all about giving your way away!

are working in my life. They are numbered, at least the first four, in order of importance. I hasten to mention that all of these points interact with each other. All seven of these "practices" should be understood as spiritual practices. I do not want to compartmentalize or separate one part of life from another. They are listed as they are for the purpose of discussion and clarification, not strict categorization.

1. Practice Devotions: *Be Spiritual*

> *Now when Daniel knew that the writing was signed, he went home. And in his upper room, with his windows open toward Jerusalem, he knelt down on his knees three times that day, and prayed and gave thanks before his God, as was his custom since early days. —Daniel 6:10*

I used to do devotions for God. I thought it made him happy. I think it does make him happy, but I've changed my way of thinking. Devotions are for me. I do them to stay "tuned in" to God and to increase spiritual awareness. My tendency is to get going in my own direction and forget about God altogether. I need a daily habit of reading, writing and praying to keep from getting lost.

Spiritual maturity is not defined by a static position with God as much as by the direction I'm headed in. Our spiritual condition has to be gauged everyday. It's not that we are spiritually insecure, but we are on a journey that demands vigilance.

The **SOAP** (**S**cripture, **O**bservation, **A**pplication and **P**rayer) method is simple and reproducible. The point is that whatever you do should be made routine; it should be a habit that keeps you in the scripture and keeps you meditating in the scripture.

For me, a daily devotional habit keeps me centered, in the middle of the merry-go-round, so to speak. All of the other disciplines depend to some degree on this first one.

2. Address Emotional Pain: *Be Vulnerable*

> *Search me, O God, and know my heart;*
> *Try me, and know my anxieties;*
> *And see if there is any hurtful way in me,*
> *And lead me in the way everlasting.* —*Psalm 139: 23-24*

Ministry is all about generating life. If I am emotionally constipated, I am no longer giving life, I am stifling it. Many people in the helping professions are people who need to be needed. They are attempting to ameliorate emotional needs through ministry. This creates confusion in the minister's life and the lives of those being served.

Whether with a close friend, a mentor, your spouse or a therapist, it is important for you to communicate your feelings. When feelings get backlogged, we lose touch with why we are

Most often
it is the ideas
that have worked
in the past that are
the greatest
impediment to
learning.
That is why
learning involves
unlearning as
much as it involves
knowledge
acquisition.

doing what we are doing and we find ourselves being compelled to do things and say things that are unclear in their intention. This kind of "disconnectedness" is common in ministry environments.

We all have to process emotional pain. Doing it honestly and deliberately will insure that ministry is pure and straightforward.

We would do well to practice emotional honesty and to help facilitate it in those close to us. A good practice is to listen carefully for emotional pain in others, let them express it, and pray for them. That's all. It is usually not necessary to analyze it, dissect it, fix it, or sermonize about it. Most feelings that arise from pain are negative, not positive. They need to be expressed and acknowledged. The more comfortable you are with your own emotions, the more at ease you will be with others.

Therapists are paid lots of money to ask people, "And how does that make you feel?" We should utilize the question more often (without charge!) and let people say how they feel, then let it go.

3. Replace Old Ideas with New Ones: *Be Teachable*

Examine me, O LORD, and prove me; Try my mind and my heart. –Psalm 26:2

Learning is not just getting new information; it is transforming and renewing our learning style, the way we learn. Learning is deeply intertwined with our emotions. To the degree that we live in fear, anxiety, depression, or anger, we are unable to learn. Keeping our minds mentally acute requires a willingness to change fundamental ideas about life. A critical yet open state of mind is facilitated by trust in God, playfulness, and a desire to grow. Learning is vitiated by the inability to recognize when good ideas, ways of thinking, or mental models have run their course.

Most often it is the ideas that have worked in the past that are the greatest impediment to learning. That is why learning involves unlearning as much as it involves knowledge acquisition.

Learning as a habit of life is much like a walk on a tightrope. On one hand it requires us to keep an open mind, to practice suspension of belief or judgment while we process new ideas. On the other, we are required to close our minds (like closing your mouth around a good sandwich) around truths that God establishes in our lives. The point is to keep the mental digestive tract moving. Our brains get accustomed to a certain rate of activity; they are trained to burn at a certain speed, like our metabolism. They can learn to learn faster, to burn more calories.

To follow Christ means to love God with "our entire mind." It means that we are not afraid of being challenged intellectually. It means that we are aware of the fleeting nature of almost everything we think we know.

To be intellectual, as I am defining it, is not about being smart, academically inclined, or "bookish." It is about being humble and reflective. It is acknowledging that God's mind transcends my current categories. *"For My thoughts are not your thoughts, nor are your ways My ways," says the LORD. For as the heavens are higher than the earth, so are My ways higher than your ways, and My thoughts than your thoughts." —Isaiah 55:8-9*

4. Manage Your Energy: *Be Physical*

"Or do you not know that your body is the temple of the Holy Spirit who is in you, whom you have from God, and you are not your own?" I Corinthians 6:19

Spiritual energy is the most significant kind of energy, but physical energy is the most fundamental. Without physical energy all of our other batteries quickly begin to drain.

Currently there is much information available on the subject of physical fitness and health. I encourage you to be a student of physical health (while not a fanatic!). I am not an expert on physical fitness but I have learned one thing: it is more important to manage your energy than to manage your time. These two are certainly not mutually exclusive, but managing your energy as opposed to merely structuring your time offers a more organic and holistic approach to prioritization than "time management" alone. When you manage your energy you are managing your time more naturally, more artlessly than trying to be too mechanical or rigid with your schedule.

First, be aware of the fact that there are seasons to everything. There are seasons of fruitfulness as well as there are seasons of winter. There are times of the year, times of the week, and times of the day when you are most productive and energetic. Examine your life and your rhythms. The trick is to synchronize your energy with your priorities. This can be done on a yearly, quarterly, weekly, daily, and even an hourly scale. "How should I spend my energy in a way that is consistent with my deepest values?"

Energy capacity diminishes both with overuse and under-use: we must balance energy expenditure with intermittent energy renewal.

Interval training is a concept that athletes are familiar with, but the idea translates into all areas of life. We gain strength and endurance when we train hard, and then rest; concentrate on a subject intensely, then back-off; pray hard and long for a season, then trust.

Here are a few suggestions from someone who almost stressed himself out to the point of losing his mind and family early in his ministry:

- Eat enough to sustain your energy for two to three hours, that's all

- Most humans require between seven and eight hours of sleep a night

- Interval training is the most effective physical exercise

- To be "fully engaged" with people and our work,

researchers say that we should take some kind of break every 90 to 120 minutes

- Recognize when you are becoming addicted to your own body chemicals, your adrenaline

- Read Dr. Archibald Hart's books on stress, male and female depression and sexuality

- Take time to allow your body to "be depressed." It needs to recover sometimes for a few days. These times of renewing may feel like "low times" emotionally. This is good and healthy.

5. Align a Team: *Be Collaborative*

"For I say, through the grace given to me, to everyone who is among you, not to think of himself more highly than he ought to think, but to think soberly, as God has dealt to each one a measure of faith. For as we have many members in one body, but all the members do not have the same function, so we, being many, are one body in Christ, and individually members of one another." I Corinthians 12: 3-5

Collaboration, according to Webster's dictionary, is the act of working together -- united labor. A strong horse can pull about 3000 pounds. Two horses can pull over 8000 pounds. To build and work as a team is to multiply, not only your efforts, but also your longevity. To work independently of others is to deny God's design for ministry. An endeavor may be fruitful for a time, but ultimately spiritual efforts that are not team oriented are doomed to failure.

Spiritual leadership is not militaristic in nature. It is not about exercising authority. It is about serving by leading. Authority is very important, but it must not be the primary source of power for a spiritual leader.

Effective team leadership aligns itself, first of all, with the larger vision of the church and its leaders. Second, it aligns itself with the members of the team – their gifts, ideas, and callings. Therefore it is important to establish two things from the outset: "Am I in the right church?" and, "Do I have the right team members?"

Both of these questions should be answered with this general rule in mind: First "Who?" then "What?" We make a fundamental commitment to our leaders and our team members by determining their integrity and values. We don't recruit people primarily by gifting, but by character.

If you have a vision of what you want to accomplish and are energized and enthusiastic about it, it is difficult to submit it to your leaders and to your team members. They may challenge it in some way. (They probably will!) But if it is a God-given vision, it will survive the scrutiny. Most importantly, if it is a God-given vision, God always has a process of assessing, sifting and testing it.

God most definitely gives us personal visions and dreams. Team ministry is the process God uses to polish the vision, removing it of all its individualistic and self-promoting edges. Ministry that has not been processed in this manner is disaster-prone. God will simply not bless a personal idol that we erect in the name of ministry.

Energy capacity diminishes both with overuse and under-use. We must balance energy expenditure with intermittent energy renewal.

6. Organize and Incorporate Your Passions:
Be Integrated

Through wisdom a house is built,

And by understanding it is established;

By knowledge the rooms are filled

With all precious and pleasant riches.

—*Proverbs 24: 3-4*

"*You can work long hours but still be slothful,*" writes Joanne Ciulla, author of *The Working Life.* "*The things that keep us from finding meaning are failure to actively engage in life and a certain laziness or lack of caring that allows us to let others make our decisions and tell us what things mean.*"

It is important that we interpret, organize, and make sense of our own lives. It is a puzzle that is unlike anyone else's. It is something that we have to take responsibility for and then put together accordingly. In many ways you cannot compare your life to anyone else's. You have to create you own "stew." There is a big difference between a shopping cart full of groceries and a gourmet meal.

The trick is to take all of the things that God puts in our cart and make a meal out of it. We have to integrate things. We have to put them together in creative ways. We have to mix up a unique "stew" of ingredients, which makes up our lives. How does our ministry relate to our family? How can we develop multi-use strategies?

If I attend a team meeting where we do devotions, share some personal issues and read a stimulating book together, I have practiced four important disciplines all in one night! If I include my family in these practices, I have integrated my life and my time by the power of ten!

"Integration" is something we should endeavor to accomplish as congregations. Ideally, we are doing devotions and reinforcing it at every turn. We are building teams and fortifying it at every level. We are creating caring communities and weaving the fabric of relationship tighter and tighter. When we do things together with the same spirit, we integrate our goals, embody a common lifestyle to new believers and, as a result, create a culture that "disciples" people almost by itself.

For the earth yields crops by itself... —Mark 4:28

A culture of discipleship creates disciples in an almost effortless way when it is done organically through integration of practices.

Integration is accomplished by combining activities, pruning activities, and constantly evaluating everything we do in light of values and vision. We do this corporately and individually. Our purpose becomes more powerful and enduring when we are evaluating it based on three questions: Are we moving from negative to positive? Are we moving from external to internal? And we moving from self to others?

7. Communicate, Communicate, Communicate:
Be Clear

> *Then the LORD answered me and said:*
> *"Write the vision*
> *And make it plain on tablets,*
> *That he may run who reads it."*
> *–Habakkuk 2:2*

Communication is the lubrication that keeps the engine purring. To communicate clearly as a leader usually means you have over-communicated to the point of exasperation. People today are receiving so many messages on a daily basis that their filters are hard to get through. They must hear something multiple times in multiple ways to really hear it once.

As our church grows and as it adjusts to doing things in a way that facilitates further growth, it will have to become better at communication at every level. Here are some practical ways to accomplish this:

- Events should be planned months in advance, not a couple of weeks

- Ministry teams should process the event together, thoroughly planning and thinking everything through

- Get the event on the church calendar as soon as possible.

- Think about how to communicate to the congregation in creative ways that do not include making announcements from the platform

- Always "debrief" every event that you do. Talk about what went well, what went not so well, what should change, and take good notes of the meeting for next time. Your team will improve its performance by leaps and bounds if you will quickly talk through an event after it has occurred.

- Repeat what is important. Talk about values. ઝ

personal response

1. In reality, what affect does a leader have on h/her people when their style reflects "having to be first" instead of "serving from the heart"? Explain.

2. We all have to process emotional pain. Doing it honestly and deliberately will insure that ministry is pure and straightforward. What happens when we allow our emotions to become "backlogged (never processing them properly)?" Explain.

3. A strong horse can pull about 3000 pounds. Two horses can pull over 8000 pounds. To build and work as a team is to multiply - what? Expound on this critical principle.

4. To become better communicators, list 3 out of the 6 things listed in this chapter that spoke to you the most. Why?

~~~~~~

speaking

Everyone has
their own ways of expression.
I believe we all have
a lot to say, but finding ways
to say it is more than half the battle.
–Criss Jami

~~~~~~

Communicating with Clarity

Demeanor • Delivery • Content

A word fitly spoken is like apples of gold in a setting of silver.

—*Proverbs 25:11*

et me preface this chapter with a statement for clarification. The communication that I am referencing here is specifically public speaking and preaching within the context of a corporate body of worship. There are solid principles of public speaking and preaching that can certainly improve personal communications. However, what I am focusing on here is the quality and impact of our words from the stage.

The weekend message is a very important event and it is probably one of the most significant public expressions of congregational values and personality.

It goes without saying that every speaker has a unique personality. God uses everyone differently. However, I want to contend for a few values and standards that apply to all of us who preach or speak publically.

There are three categories: Demeanor, Delivery, and Content.

DEMEANOR

Our demeanor is important and we often don't put enough thought into it. Demeanor means the way one behaves towards others or carries one's self: one's bearing or appearance. It could be mistaken for 'body language' but that wouldn't be quite accurate. Demeanor is the reflection of an inner attitude and it speaks volumes before we ever open our mouth or utter a sound. It is the outward expression of our personal mindset and it reflects our most deeply internalized attitudes and beliefs. Demeanor sends powerful messages to listeners and viewers that either gives credibility to what we are going to say, or discredits us as a trusted authority before we can establish that trust.

HERE ARE SOME CORE ELEMENTS TO STRENGTHENING YOUR DEMEANOR

- *Know Where You Stand With God Before You Step Up To Microphone.* Everything you feel, think, say and model stems from your practical knowledge of where you stand with God and where you don't. This is of primary importance. How we carry ourselves is based on deeply internalized knowledge and its forthcoming beliefs about one's position with God and with others. Make a conscious practice of acknowledging the truth about your relationship with Him and the conditions that you have been freed from as a child of God. For some of us it takes literal rehearsal of essential truths before they can be fully remembered and incorporated. Be clear about this so it comes through you without thinking.

- *Respect Your Hearers.* This is the next most important thing to remember. In an attempt to be authoritative, we may unintentionally "speak down" to our audience. Big mistake! When making a negative point we may use "we" or "I" but not "you." There are many preachers who do this all the time. Some churches are trained to

---— ❦ ———

People know
when you like
them and
when they
are accepted.
To like your
audience is a great
protection against
speaking down to
them but also
gives everyone a
strong dose of
grace that can be
given back to you
should you miss
your mark here
and there.

---

expect scolding and reprimand. They don't think they've been to church unless the preacher "dresses them down." This is an unhealthy and immature practice. It creates co-dependent followers besides being unbecoming and juvenile.

- **Like Your Audience.** Deliberately deciding and setting yourself to like your audience creates an unspoken climate of welcome and it allows both you and those in the audience an immediate environment to feel safe in. People know when you like them and when they are accepted. To like your audience is a great protection against speaking down to them but also gives everyone a strong dose of grace that can be given back to you should you miss your mark here and there. It brings an critical element of emotional warmth and receptivity which in turns allows for greater learning and exchange.

- *Use Intensity Wisely.* It is good to be intense, but if you use an exclamation mark after every sentence it becomes monotonous and irritating. If you have something to say, then the content of your message will speak for itself. It is not necessary to "push" all your material at the congregation. They are intelligent. They will get it. Be passionate, but like good comedy or great romance, restrain your energy for the right moments.

- *Let Humor Inform Your Message.* If you take yourself too seriously, at best the congregation will find you amusing, privately snicker at you, and dismiss your message. At worst, they will find you boring and tune you out. Your message will not be heard. Many preachers think that to be authoritative they must be extremely serious and "fatherly." Most people see right through this kind of posturing and are turned off to it. Be yourself and let God inhabit the message as you deliver it. You don't need to help God by being "preacher-esque." It takes

years of ministry and some gray hairs to be a father figure. Speak with authority because God has given it to
you, but don't come off stilted or false as a cover up for
the authority you are meant to walk in freely and hum-
bly. Humor will allow you to stay more relaxed and help
to prevent you from sliding into pretentious posturing.

- *Don't Apologize For Who You Are, What You Are Going
  To Say Or The Occasion Of Your Speaking.* There is no
  quicker way of turning off everyone's ears than to wal-
  low in false humility or to denigrate your message before
  you've given it. Stand up and deliver!

- *Never, Never, Never Express Personal Irritation Or
  Frustration With The Congregation In Your Preaching.*
  Never allow personal frustration or anger to seep into
  your message. Our job is to inspire, teach, and encourage. I should deal with people who are frustrating me
  one-on-one, not from the platform. Sometimes it is necessary before I speak to get centered on God and
  remind myself that this opportunity to preach is not
  about me in any sense. IT IS ALL ABOUT HIM AND
  ALL ABOUT EDIFYING HIS PEOPLE.

- *Use Positive Persuasion, Not Negative "Guilting."*
  Using guilt is a lazy preacher's devise. It's a shortcut
  for creating short-term results. Guilt is appropriate

when it arises naturally from the context of scripture, but be very careful! This is best used in context of private conversation over specific matters and where direct follow through is possible. It is too easy to slip into using guilt as a devise to change our hearers because we haven't prayed enough or been thoughtful enough about our words. Be intelligent and spiritually incisive; not brash and confrontational.

DELIVERY

Delivery describes specific style that you give your message to the audience and could be likened to how you wrap a gift. Dramatic, understated, highly emotional, intensely personal, emotionally detached but intellectually engaged all are descriptions of delivery style. Whether you are free-preaching; preaching from memory; extemporaneously; or reading your notes, the ultimate goal is to deliver a life-giving message that will be heard and received by the congregation. Delivery style requires continued practice to improve but there are a few essentials I want to establish here as the basics for good preaching and public speaking.

A core element of delivery is body language. Body language is how we move, our posture, the fullness of our eye contact, the tone of our voice. Be mindful of how and what you are com-

municating without words to emphasize the impact the believability of your spoken message.

- *Be conversational, not oratorical.* Listen and learn from
  effective communicators in the media. No one uses an oratorical style. "Oratory" is a left-over approach from the
  nineteenth century. It comes across extremely backwards
  to anyone but dyed-in-the-wool church people. Whether
  Colin Powell or John Madden, contemporary communicators use a natural and informal delivery style.

- *Your visual presence counts for much of your credibility.*
  Researchers like Albert Mehrabian have discovered that
  our verbal content is often smothered by the vocal and
  visual components of our message. According to him,
  believability is determined by verbal content (7%), vocal
  tone and quality (38%) and visual presentation (55%).

- *Eye communication is your number one tool for connecting
  with people.* Let your team critique you on this. You can
  do many things right, but if you are weak at engaging
  people with your eyes and expression, they will not
  deem you to be a convincing.

- *Make sure you energy level is always moderately high.* If
  your energy level dips too low, you will lose your audience. Sometimes energy is maintained with a pause or a

gesture or a whisper or a shout. Learn a wide range of "energy" sustainers. If you depend on just a couple, they will become less effective.

- **Don't try to hit home-runs.** This is especially important if you are an occasional preacher. The congregation will sense that you are trying too hard. Aim for a solid double, or a couple of base hits. Organize your material wisely and don't try to say every great thing you've thought of the last few months.

- **Don't flatter or charm yourself to the congregation.** If you are not

Prepare thoroughly and pray through your message. Then get up, relax and let God do what you can't do alone with all the preparation in the world.

ther primary leader of the congregation but a "member-of-the-team preacher", you are to represent the pastor and the pastoral team. This should be a tangible point of realization for the congregation. They should feel that they have heard from God and their pastor no matter who speaks to them. This is especially important for those of us who are on staff together. My point is that as a member of the pastoral team, try to harmonize with the other members of the preaching team.

CONTENT

Demeanor and delivery can be dazzling but if your content is light the congregation will feel they're being sold fluff instead of being given substance. And they'll be right. Packaging matters but you still have to have something in the package and it has to have real value.

Here are a few basics to remember about developing and delivering content.

- *Have one theme and use it as a clothesline.* Hang all your points on one basic idea. If your theme is as strong as it should be, the order of your points will not be that important.

- *Be thematic and expositional at the same time.* Preach directly from the scripture, but present a clear point of view immediately. Let everyone know where you are going. Ask a pointed and practical question, for instance, and then proceed to answer it.

- *Always ask, "so what?" Of everything you prepare.* Get to the concrete point quickly. Don't ruminate and theorize very much. People are always asking "So what?" so you should ask this question as you prepare. You should not display your technical knowledge or reveal your study methods to the congregation. They don't care. Get to the material issue.

- *Use exposition, logic, and emotion.* If you only use one of these approaches, you will be less convincing. People learn in different ways. Make a point from a couple of directions. You are speaking to the believer and the unbeliever, the romantic and the pragmatist, the "feeler" and the thinker.

- *Try to create a tie-in with the current theme or series that your church is in.* This will lend you credibility with the congregation and reinforce an important value: that you are not just individual preachers, but a team of people hearing God together and providing leadership accordingly.

- *As a general rule, don't tell jokes.* Let your humor be a natural part of your presentation. Along these lines, don't let an illustration be the dominating image. In other words, don't' let the tail wag the dog. An illustration should serve the theme and the text, it shouldn't overshadow it. Sometimes I will forego a powerful movie clip or story if it overpowers the substance of the message or if it elicits questions and issues I'm not prepared to address.

- *And finally: preach on what you know.* Stay within yourself; don't over-reach. Your listeners will know it immediately and tune you out. Cut everything back to the heart. Preach on what you have really ingested into your life and keep it simple. People will likely remember one thing you say, so be careful to speak with this in mind.

It is amazing how much we reveal about ourselves when we preach. Folks can see right through us! This is scary but this is also our opportunity. Be real. Be straight. Be honest. Be humble. Be appropriate. Be yourself.

Prepare thoroughly and pray through your message. Then get up, relax and let God do what you can't do alone with all the preparation in the world. ☙

personal
response

1. What are the 3 categories that apply to all of us who preach or speak publically? Which 1 of the 3 do you perceive you'll have a challenge with? If any, explain why.

2. Before you step up to the microphone to speak/teach/preach, what can you say is your greatest fear you need to overcome? What is your plan to face that fear and beat it?

3. Describe your ministry style (your delivery method).

4. In retrospect, what is one of the worst memories of a message you delivered? Explain why you think it went so bad.

5. In retrospect, what is one of the best memories of a message you delivered? Explain why you think it went so well.

6. It is amazing how much we reveal about ourselves when we preach. Folks can see right through us! This is scary but this is also our opportunity to: Be real. Be straight. Be honest and be _____. (Fill in blank).

Who I am
forms and defines what I do.
What I do
forms and defines who I am,
creating my identity.

When I am vulnerable
in my community
and disciplined
in my reflection,
I can be assured of continually
becoming who I am.

When I stabilize my actions
with a deep sense
of spiritual identity,
I will be selective
and focused.

When I actualize
'who I am'
with purposeful behavior,
I will feel energized
and empowered.

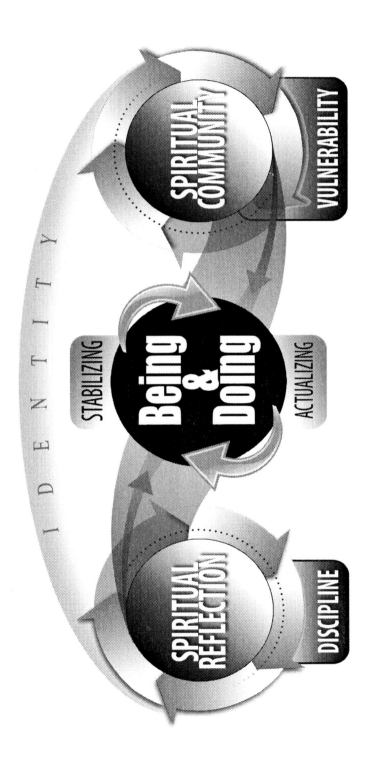

endnotes

1. Bronowski, J. (1973) *The Ascent of Man*, BBC Books, United Kingdom: p.i.

2. Tillich, P. (1952). *The Courage to Be*. Yale University: pp. 163-166.

3. Nouwen, H.J.M. (1989). *In The Name of Jesus: Reflections on Christian Leadership*. Crossroad Pub. Co.: p. 28.

4. Spurgeon, C. H.(1954). *Lectures to My Students*. Zondervan: p. 7.

5. Buechner, F. (1983). *Now and Then*. Harper & Row: p. 87, 92.

6. Kierkegaard, S. (1938). *Purity of Heart*. Harper & Row: p. 140.

7. Bonhoeffer, D. (1954). *Life Together: The Classic Exploration of Faith in Community*. Harper & Row: p. 29..:

8. Sempangi, F. K. (2006). *A Distant Grief: The Real Story Behind the Martyrdom of Christians in Uganda*. Wipf & Stock Pub.: p. 187.

9. Dillard, A. (1982). *Teaching a Stone to Talk: Expeditions and Encounters*. Harper Perennial: pp. 85-94.

10. Friedman, E. (1985). *Generation to Generation; Family Process in Church and Synagogue*. Guilford Press: p. 183

11. In *Creating Minds: An Anatomy of Creativity Seen Through the Lives of Freud, Einstein, Picasso*, et al., (Harper Collins, 1993), Howard Gardner argues that the 'creators' in his book made their contributions to their disciplines after roughly ten years of tireless dedication to mastering them, combined with the courage and brilliance to

challenge them. Could there be a lesson for us here? Is it possible that imitation precedes originality? 'Pushing away from the pack' may be foolish for the naive or the young, inexperienced pastor. Never to 'push away' in some form or another, however, would certainly be a pity. Indeed, Gardner observes, "it would be unwarranted to contend that one first follows the craft for ten years and one then strikes out on one's own . . . Individuals who ultimately make creative breakthroughs tend, from the earliest days, to be explorers, innovators, tinkerers."

12. In *The Making of a Leader,* (NavPress, 1988), Robert Clinton discusses 'leadership backlash.' "The leadership backlash process item refers to the negative reaction of followers, other leaders within the group, and Christians outside the group to a course of action taken by a leader once ramifications develop from the decision." He sets forth this pattern:

1. The leader gets a vision (direction) from God.
2. The followers are convinced of the direction.
3. The group moves in the direction given.
4. The group experiences persecution, hard times, or attacks from Satan. Spiritual warfare is common.
5. There is backlash from the group.
6. The leader is driven to God to seek affirmation in spite of the actions ramifications.
7. God reveals Himself further–who He is, what He intends to do. He makes it clear that He will deliver.
8. God vindicates Himself and the leader.

13. Ciulla, J.B, (2000) *The Working Life: The Promise and Betrayal of Modern Work,* Three Rivers Press: NY

To contact author

Please go to:

www.GatewayCollegium.com